Lessons Not Learned in School

Myndel Miller

Copyright © 2021 Myndel Miller

All rights reserved. This book or any portion thereof may not be reproduced or used in any manner whatsoever without the express written permission of the publisher except for the use of brief quotations in a book review.

ISBN: 978-1-7362141-1-4

Printed in the United States of America

First Printing, 2021

Dedication

This book is for every student in this school called life—may this book make it just a little more manageable for you.

CONTENTS

Introduction - Before the Book 1
CHAPTER 1 - Your Stuff and Other People's Stuff 3
CHAPTER 2 - The Competitive Comparison 7
CHAPTER 3 - You're Not Going to Like Everyone—Get Over It. 13
CHAPTER 4 - The Skin You're In...17
CHAPTER 5 - The Cookie Conversation..19
CHAPTER 6 - Hello 25
CHAPTER 7 - Use Money—Don't Worship It. 27
CHAPTER 8 - What Is Your Problem?...29
CHAPTER 9 - Get Smart 33
CHAPTER 10 - N*gga 35
CHAPTER 11 - Learn How to (and not to) Give to Others........................37
CHAPTER 12 - Cars in Cash 39
CHAPTER 13 - More Books, Less Boobs and Butt 43
CHAPTER 14 - Never, Never, Never Give Up 45
CHAPTER 15 - Mission Control..49
CHAPTER 16 - Gratitude and Gutter Greetings 53
CHAPTER 17 - Dark and Different 57
CHAPTER 18 - Harvest Time 61
CHAPTER 19 - House, Sweet House..65
CHAPTER 20 - Moms, Dads and Other Grown Folk.............................69
CHAPTER 21 - The Fear Factor...73
CHAPTER 22 - Processions, Prisons, and Pens 75
CHAPTER 23 - Cruising and Caring for Self... 81
CHAPTER 24 - Bills, Borrowing, and Being Bossed 83
CHAPTER 25 - Baby Mama Aspirations 87
CHAPTER 26 - The 'tude, the Trunk, and the Inappropriate Touch 91
CHAPTER 27 - Friends, Fault-Finding, Fads, and Fathers 97
CHAPTER 28 - Matters of the Heart..103
CHAPTER 29 - Coins, Kids, Communication, and College......................109
CHAPTER 30 - Amazing Life, Amazing You 115
Discussion Questions.. 119

Introduction
Before the Book

    Six years ago, I published my very first book. Before then, writing a book—becoming an author—had just been a desire, a thought. It was something I had been wanting to do for quite a while. At that time, I was in my twenty-second year of teaching, and was working with high school students—seniors, to be exact. The course I taught was a reading class for students who had not yet been able to pass the state's standardized test for graduation. No pressure, right? Fortunately, for those students and for me, it was not my first time teaching the course. I say this, because you can imagine how a student must feel to be in their senior year of high school with this test that they had been taking repeatedly since tenth grade still hanging over their head. I say it was fortunate for them, because unlike my first year of teaching the course with little to no direction from anyone (including the state), I had decided to approach things in a manner that felt a little less like teaching to the test. I had a better handle on how to calm students' fears surrounding graduation and their ability to earn a diploma. I was better able to calm their anxieties about possibly earning a Certificate of Completion, which would mean that while they had completed the necessary coursework for graduation, they were a test (or two) short of earning the coveted diploma. I say it was fortunate for me, because knowing what I was doing from a teaching standpoint, that year, freed me up to begin writing down the things I had been wanting to share with students about life.

I entered the field of education as a third-grade teacher, and, even then, it was important to me that students learn, not just the academics that were a part of the curriculum, but the life lessons that would carry them into adulthood. I can remember teaching financial literacy to my fifth graders, because who doesn't need to learn about money? And the sooner, the better! So, that year with those seniors, some of the life lessons I knew they would need kept coming to me, and while I devoted some class time to discussing certain things with them, there simply wasn't enough time in our days together to even come close to sharing everything I wanted them to know before they left high school.

And that's how the idea for my first book came about. By day, I was a teacher to about 150 students, I was the head of the Reading and English Departments, I was a lead mentor to teachers new to the school and/or to the profession, and there were a few other positions I held that year that I don't recall now, and then by night, I was writing a book. Once the book *Before You Leave, I Just Want to Say...* was published, I began receiving feedback from adults as well as from young people, and the adults were letting me know that the information was helpful for them, too—hence, my decision to republish and include some additional content. Here comes the first lesson, and please note that these are not in any special order:

CHAPTER 1
Your Stuff and Other People's Stuff

Work on Your Stuff, Too.

The vast majority of us who have a job, or who have a career in a particular field, work for somebody else, which is cool as long as that continues to satisfy you. Some people are perfectly okay with working for someone else and will work a job until they are ready for retirement, should they be afforded the opportunity. If you work with someone like that, you may hear them complain about the job from time to time—the pay, the boss, the other employees, the commute, the customers—but they will continue to show up for work each day. And that's okay! You can have a fulfilling life while working for an organization or for a particular company or corporation. But then, there are other people—a group much smaller in number—who want a little more. These people dream of having their own business, they dream of living their life on their own terms, they dream of setting their own schedules, and of calling the shots, so to speak.

I saw someone's social media post the other day, stating that schools are only preparing our young to work for other people—to be someone's employee rather than to have businesses of their own. And while I am not here to support nor to refute their claim, I will venture to say that most school districts, if not all of them, do include some sort of employability skills as a part of their curriculum. Students are taught that going to school is their first job, and they are taught about the importance of being present, being on time, following the rules, working well with others, and producing quality work, to name a few of those skills. By the way, the same behaviors expected of students on school campuses are also expected of adults in the workplace—just in case some of you, young ones, thought you'd be rid of those pesky expectations once you moved into adulthood. Cursing out your boss is no more accepted from grown folk on the job than it is from unruly students in a classroom, so take heed to those employability skills.

Now, if you are one of those people who hopes to, one day, have your own business, then knowing what it takes to make a good employee will help you in becoming your own boss. Each one of those skills will need to become habit for you, because being your own boss, also, means being your own employee. I'll wait. Did you catch that? I'll say it again in a different way: If you work for yourself, you are your own employee. And what kind of person do you want showing up to your job? Somebody with a bad attitude? (We'll talk more about that later.) And how do you want them showing up? Late half of the time, and not with the proper tools for the job? My guess is that you will want them to adhere to all of the policies explained in the employee handbook; or, in other words, possess the aforementioned employability skills. Why? Because those are the skills that will help your business to operate successfully.

Something that is important to note here is that while you are working for someone else, you should try to learn all you can about how business is conducted. *But I work at a fast-food restaurant, and that's not what I want to do with my life.* You're missing the point, so let me help you. While working at that fast-food restaurant you don't like, you work with customers every day—nice customers, cranky customers, rude customers, and complaining customers. Working with all kinds of customers has taught you how to deal with all kinds of people—some of the same kinds of people that you will, no doubt, interact with when you have a business of your own. Do you see how that works? This means that none of the time you spend working for someone else should be considered wasted time. Yes, you are developing a plan for your departure, but in the meanwhile you are, also, preparing by learning valuable lessons and skills from that same job you want to leave. Students, it's the same thing with school. Maybe what can be learned from the Math or English class you detest, is how to push through a challenge and come out on the other side of it—how to not give up at the first sign of a struggle. And if that were all you were able to take away from the experience—whew, Chile—you would have learned a valuable lesson indeed. You might not want to be where you are, but while you are there choose to learn all you can for the next leg of your journey. Enough said. I hope.

  While you are working for someone else, do not neglect to set aside time to work on your stuff, too. People who are close to me have heard me say something to this effect: *For the next two hours, I'll be working on something for the district*, meaning that I will be completing some task for my current employer in my profession as a teacher. This implies that there are times when I work for me. I can say with absolute certainty that I am and have always been an excellent employee for any organization that employed me. A good work ethic is something my parents did a great job of modeling for me, and it has served me well. If I need to go in early to accomplish a task, I do it. If I need to stay later to make it happen, I do that. I am now at a place in my profession where I have accumulated personal and sick days off with pay. As a teacher who would very seldom be absent from the classroom, I had and still do have quite a collection of these days.

I have learned that it's important for me to work on my business, too. I have learned that that job will keep on going without me; in fact, if something were to happen to me, a vacancy for my position would be posted in no time and prospective employees would be scheduling appointments with the school's administration for an interview. I have also seen that when a job is ready to get rid of you, they will very politely explain to you that they have decided to *go in a different direction* which is code in the professional world for *we no longer need you*. So, yes, depending on what I am working on for myself, I may need to take some time away from that other job to be able to do it. Even though you may not be able to take a day off from your job, you must still do your very best to put aside some time for working on the building of your business. Find the time. Prioritize the time. It is easy to get so caught up in working to build someone else's business that you never get around to building your own. I will say it again: Work on your stuff, too.

CHAPTER 2
The Competitive Comparison

Don't Compare Yourself to Others and Here's Why.

Speaking of other people's stuff: There will always be someone prettier, stronger, more handsome, richer, better educated, taller, thinner, faster and any other -*er* you can think of, according to society's standards anyway, so to compare yourself to others is not a wise thing to do. It seems that women, especially, have been conditioned by society to hold certain physical characteristics in high regard. Those characteristics are what we use to judge ourselves—rather harshly, I might add—and then, we turn around and judge other women by the same ridiculous standards. Weight is by far the most often used measuring stick, and then there's hair texture and length, body shape, breast size, butt size, complexion and the disturbing list goes on.

Males do compare themselves to other males, but I don't believe it is to the extent that females do it. As you grow older, young sir, you'll be more likely to find yourself looking at your peers and comparing what they're driving to what you're driving, or where they're living as compared to where you're living, or what they do for a living and how much they earn versus what you do and earn. I believe that at some point in your life, even if you don't look to see how you stack-up according to society's standards, you will (at the very least) look around at the people within your circle to see how you measure up. As you're scrolling through social media land, you will look at who earned a college degree versus who joined the workforce right after high school, and how successful they seem to be; you'll look at your circle's relationship statuses to see who is in a great relationship versus who has drama or who is in no relationship at all.

A certain amount of comparison is natural, I suppose, but what I caution you against doing is living your life as though you're in a competition with others. That kind of competitive comparison can make you feel somehow better than the next person when life is going well. It can lead to you being really down on yourself—feeling as though you're not as good as the next person, or that you are somehow behind in life when things are not going as well. It can even result in you becoming a hater, and we don't want that, do we? Of course, we don't. But let's face it, when it looks like life is happening for everyone around you—college acceptance letters, first apartment, new job, new car, exotic vacation, a new house, a new boyfriend/girlfriend, an accepted marriage proposal—and not for you, it can leave you feeling bummed. Really bummed.

Let me show you how you can be genuinely happy when things happen for your friends and for other people in your circle. Just remember this: Everything comes with a price. Everything. For example, you may see someone driving a Benz, and you say to yourself *Man, I wish I had one*, but what you don't know is that that person is struggling to make the payment each month, or perhaps they made some sacrifices that you may be unwilling to make to get what they have—they saved their money, they worked longer hours on the job, they stopped ordering stuff online every other day (you know who you are), they invested time in their own business resulting in an additional stream of income. Know that there was a cost somewhere along the way because everything comes with a price. You want that muscular physique? It looks good, doesn't it? Well, the price for that banging body is the discipline of an exercise regimen and healthy eating. You want the better-paying job? The price is it comes with more responsibility and may require more schooling. You want to pass that test? The price is putting in some serious, uninterrupted study time instead of checking your phone every two minutes. You want the relationship they appear to have? So, first of all, she's not that nice behind closed doors, and that brother is having a hard time. Or maybe they are both really cool people, but please know that life for them ain't peaches and cream every day. Don't let those social media posts fool you—people are out there paying prices!

It's been quite some time now since I ran into this couple—a husband and wife—that I'd not seen in a few years. The husband almost immediately informed me that they were (at the time) living in a big house. No, seriously, he asked me "How have you been?" and before the response had left my lips, he told me, "Well, you know, we bought this big house." His exact words. Wow. *Okay*, I thought to myself. I said something along the lines of "Oh, that is so good"—and I meant every word of it—and then I chuckled to myself, and in my mind, I shook my head. I chuckled (and shook my head) because he felt the need to tell me about his house, of all things. I had not seen him in years, and that was what he greeted me with? Interesting, huh? He clearly wanted me to know he had a house, and it was big.

I chuckled, too, because I'm a homeowner; in fact, the house I live in now is the sixth house I've purchased up to this point in my life. And hopefully, you understand I share this with you for two reasons only: the first being to make it clear that I wasn't hating on that couple; and the second, and most important, is so you'll know that owning a home is most definitely within the realm of possibility for you, if you so desire. You can have that. I want for every person reading this book to feel that way—and while I want women to feel empowered to purchase a home, I especially want to encourage young men to do so. I don't know that home ownership is as common among young men, and I would like to see a shift in that area. There will be more on that later.

For the past ten years, I have owned three properties—one is my place of residence and the other two serve as rental properties. So, when I think of homeownership, my mind automatically goes to two places; one of which is the costs involved in maintaining a house. Buying a house is one thing—maintaining it is quite another. When you are the owner (of anything), the buck always stops with you. *Something breaks?* That's on you. *A mortgage payment due?* You. *Is the roof leaking?* Yeah, that's you, too. I walked away that day wondering if that couple had yet lived through a Florida summer of having to cool a big house, and then I chuckled again. I was, and am, genuinely happy for them, because I understand the price that goes along with owning a home, and that keeps me from comparing to the point of hating. Oftentimes, when we see others with material possessions or we see others who have attained a certain status in life, we want what they have; what we fail to realize, though, is that those possessions and the status come at a price. There is a price to be paid for those things, and it's not always a monetary price. You want to be the next NBA phenom, but you don't want to practice—it doesn't work like that, folks. Practicing your three-point shots while your friends are turning up at a party doing shots is the price you may have to pay. Everything comes with a price. Everything. The other place my mind automatically goes when I think of homeownership is income potential, but we will talk about this later.

I suppose that another lesson to learn here is that while

you're minding your own business, somebody somewhere might be watching you and comparing themselves to you so much that they have likened themselves to being in a competition with you. And you don't even know it! Well, not until they say something like the big-house-guy did. People don't just trip in high school—some people continue tripping well into adulthood.

Here's one more way to keep from comparing yourself to others: Learn how to be content with what you have. Learn to be grateful for what you have. I am not telling you not to desire more—I would never do that—but I am telling you to look at what you already have and be thankful for it. I know people who are so busy looking at what others have, and at what others are doing, that they are completely missing out on how fortunate they are. Or they're so busy being focused on what they don't have that they're not appreciating all the good that is in their life.

Your life may not be all you want it to be right now but trust me when I tell you that there is always someone worse off than you. While you're complaining about your curly hair and how it tangles up after you wash it, there's someone who just wishes they had some hair. While you're complaining about your Mom and her nagging, there's someone who would give anything to see theirs again. When you open your mouth to complain about how much homework you need to do, there is a young person somewhere that would love to be in school. When you open your mouth (again) to complain about your boss and about your job, there is somebody who would be grateful for that job and gladly learn to get along with that difficult supervisor. I'm serious! What we take for granted, and even complain about, would mean the whole world to someone else—and I'm not talking about in some third-world country somewhere either! There are people that you come into contact with every day, who would love to have your life, because theirs is so tough—they're homeless, they're being abused, they're hungry, they're ill. So, don't compare yourself to others, because you'll be comparing apples to oranges. You just run the race you need to run; stop looking with envy at the next person's lane. They may be running the 50-yard dash while you're running a marathon—two totally different types of races that require two totally different approaches and techniques for finishing. Do your best to succeed at running your own race.

CHAPTER 3
You're Not Going to Like Everyone—Get Over It.

And here's a newsflash for you: Not everyone is going to like you either. As adults, we don't get to only deal with the people we like and who like us back. No. Real, mature adults sometimes need to *man up* and *woman up* and *suck it up* to get the job done and to get along in life. As respectfully as possible, deal with people—even the difficult ones—the way you would want someone dealing with you. Depending on who I'm interacting with, I may have to constantly remind myself to view that person as though they are somebody's child. And they are, so I treat them with the basic respect I would want for my child, or for my parents. You don't have to love 'em, but the much-needed civility our society seems to be lacking requires it.

As a classroom teacher for so many years, I can't tell you how many times I have heard *That teacher doesn't like me.* Oh, if only I had a dollar for all the times that I heard that one. That phrase would usually rear its ugly head when I sat down with students, one-on-one, to look at their grades in my class as well as in their other classes.

My response usually went something like this: She/he may not like you, but guess what? They have some information that you need, and so long as they are not withholding that knowledge from you, whether they like you is irrelevant. Totally irrelevant.

What will you do when your boss doesn't like you? Or how about they do like you, but they don't believe you're the one for the promotion? Huh? What will you do? I'll tell you what you'll do—your job! Where did you get the impression you have to like, and be liked, to do a job? Who told you that? They lied. Look, it's a beautiful thing when your teacher/professor/employer/mother-in-law actually cares about you, but it is not a prerequisite to you doing what you need to do. You better learn to like yourself. You better learn to appreciate yourself. To use common vernacular: Chile, please! Nobody has to like you. Go to school and pay attention in your classes. Go to work and do the job you are being paid to do. Like you? Chile, please. But then again, perhaps, they would like you, if you didn't spend half of the class or half the time during your shift trying to sneak a text (I'll talk about that in greater detail later).

And where did we get the impression that just because we don't like someone, we should make disparaging comments to them, or about them to others? In recent times, so-called adults appear to be the biggest offenders where this is concerned. If only members of different political parties could just get along. I guess the fact that our youngest and most impressionable people are witnessing these rants, isn't enough to cause you to be civil? Having been fortunate enough to have lived for more than half of a century, while folks my age and younger are no longer here, I better understand the brevity and fragility of human life. None of us knows when the moment we're in, will be the last moment. Is calling someone else names really the way you want to spend your time? I think not.

And another thing: You don't have to like a person to learn from them. I had some students one year not long after my switch from elementary school to high school who had to learn that lesson. During those days, I was teaching that Reading course I mentioned earlier, and I had a mix of grade levels in each of my classes—sophomores, juniors, seniors, and even the occasional freshman in the same class. I know the subject was the same, but the objective, my approach, and the materials were different depending on the grade level. On most days, I was a black, modern-day Laura Ingalls Wilder in a one-room schoolhouse disguised as a portable. Depending on how old you are as you read this, you have no idea who I am referring to, and have missed an opportunity to laugh out loud. Oh, well. I'm sure I'll make some other reference along the way that you will understand.

In one of those classes, I had three young men who were seniors and who were preparing to take one of those standardized tests used for college admissions, because a high enough score on the reading portion would satisfy the reading test that was a state requirement for high school graduation. There was another teacher who had a proven track record of successfully preparing students to do well on the exam, and she was able to work with my three as she had a small number of students in her own classroom at that time who were preparing for the same test, and she offered to include mine. This was great, because she was better able to focus on what they needed at that time, leaving me to work with my larger group on different content. A win for everybody, right?

After a few times of sending my students to her, she stopped by my portable one day during planning to share some concerns; apparently, my three young men had been giving her a hard way to go. That news surprised me—these young men always treated me with the utmost respect—but I needed to address the behaviors they were exhibiting during her class. I was disappointed that they had chosen not to take full advantage of this time to focus on the task at hand. Couldn't they see that they were shooting themselves in the foot, figuratively speaking, of course? That report from her ticked me off, because that colleague was doing me a favor, she was doing them a favor, and their being disrespectful to her was just plain wrong. What bothered me most of all was the fact that they were allowing how they felt about this teacher, about the situation, about whatever to keep them from gaining what this teacher had to offer.

Most people would describe me as mild-mannered, and I am, but when I become angry there is a different kind of calm that I exude—I don't yell, though my voice can sometimes become elevated; I don't use profanity, because that's not my thing, but my words in that moment are exact and precise in getting my point across. My eyebrows are definitely furrowed, and I'm squinting my eyes as my mind tries desperately to comprehend why something was said or done. I vividly recall sitting with these three males at the counter-height dining room set I'd bought and assembled for my classroom, thinking that sitting there would bear less of a stigma when meeting with me for small-group instruction. I can recall their faces as I quietly but firmly gave them the business; asking them questions they knew were very much rhetorical, then watching them hang their heads during the silent moments of our one-sided conversation. I shared with them, then, what I'm sharing with you: Do not let you not liking someone, keep you from getting what you need from them. And by the same token, do not let someone else's dislike for you, keep you from getting what you need from them.

By the way, all three young men adjusted their behavior in the other teacher's classroom, and went on to earn the score needed to obtain their diplomas.

CHAPTER 4
The Skin You're In

Save the Skin.

My fair-skinned readers, you may want to just talk amongst yourselves for a moment. Wait... is ashy skin even an issue for you? I'm not sure. Oh, well. Seriously though, all skin types need to guard against dryness. It has been my experience that lotion just doesn't quite cut it when it comes to fighting against dry, ashy skin. Might I suggest you give petroleum jelly a try? It comes in a jar as well as in a tube. I know many of you are probably turning up your noses at this bit of advice, but don't knock it until you've tried it. Lol. I bet you my fifty-one-year-old skin is softer than the skin of many a thirty-seven-year-old, or even a seventeen-year-old. Look, I know it doesn't smell like strawberries, or whatever scent you are accustomed to, but it protects your skin.

Whether you decide to try the petroleum jelly, or you decide to continue using lotion, you definitely need to apply one of those to your skin shortly after getting out of the shower, or bathtub. You'll be less ashy if your skin is still moist during the application of whichever product you decide to use. I have used it on my limbs and torso since I was a child, and it has served me well. Man, woman, boy, and girl—human beings—pay, at least, this much attention to your skin. Tell you what—use the petroleum jelly then top it off with some lotion. How's that for a little skin-care compromise? Do something. This is the only skin you'll receive, so care for it.

Your Hands and Feet, Sirs.

Gentlemen, please, clip those fingernails and do not house dirt underneath them. Guys need to take care of their hands and feet, too. Not necessarily a manicure/pedicure—although there is nothing wrong with a guy getting those—but clip those talons and slap some petroleum jelly (or lotion) on those puppies. And give your heels some attention, too, especially if you are one of those people who likes to walk about without wearing shoes or socks. There's this thing called a pumice stone that can be used to rid your heels of calloused skin. Your feet are a part of your body and need to be cared for, too. (You're welcome, ladies.)

CHAPTER 5
The Cookie Conversation

I have always hoped that my students would wait—the young men, too—until they're a good twenty-five years old (or how about married?!) before deciding to knock boots—that was one of the slang terms for sex when I was in high school. I never quite understood it, because no one I knew wore boots and I certainly did not own a pair. And were they talking about cowboy boots? Anyway, for the seniors I had six years ago, one of the slang terms they had for having sex was smashing. Eew. Who comes up with these terms? That just sounds wrong—who, in their right mind, would want to engage in anything called smashing? Look, if I had my way, none of my students would have been having sex. As adults, who have been around for a minute, I'm sure most would agree that there is far more to sex than meets the eye. There are a lot of emotions and responsibilities that go along with engaging in sexual activity that, I dare say, even some adults are not fully prepared to deal with.

Here's my advice to young people when it comes to sex—hereby referred to as the cookie (I heard that term used once in a movie and find it to be a kinder, gentler term.): Young people, hold on to your cookie. Keep the lid on the cookie jar. Don't be so quick to share it. And beware of the cookie monsters! You're probably laughing, but I'm so serious. Cookie monsters are people, who are solely interested in... well, cookies. They don't care about who you are as a person. They don't want to know about your aspirations in life. They don't want to be your friend, though, they may befriend you (or even boyfriend, or girlfriend you) to get the cookie... and a cookie once shared can't be unshared.

I've been a woman for a little while now, and I can tell you that most of us are pretty emotional beings—not that men don't have emotions, because they absolutely do! It's just that women are definitely more in touch with their feelings than men are with theirs. For most of us women, when we really like a guy and we believe he likes us, we have the tendency to want to give to him. We will cook meals for him, buy him a gift on his birthday, give him the answers to an assignment, give him a back rub, the use of our car, the use of our credit card, and the benefit of the doubt (even if in our heart of hearts, we know he doesn't treat us right and we deserve better). We will give him our heart. We may even give him the cookie.

Now, when we, as women, decide to share the cookie, we are giving a part of ourselves that is, it seems, directly connected to our heart. I don't know how the cookie is connected to the heart of a woman—I just know it is. Sex is not just a physical act for us. For plenty of women, intimacy at that level means commitment and a future together. So, for a guy to receive the cookie and then walk away, or refuse to answer texts, or decide to share details about the cookie with his friends, or move on to sample other cookies—well, that can break a young woman's heart. Truth be told, it can break a grown woman's heart.

During my first year of teaching high school students, I taught in a classroom with two doors. At one end of the room was a door that led to a courtyard; the door at the other end of the room was locked at all times and considered to be the back door and was to only be used for exiting the classroom. All of my students knew not to knock on that back door, because I was not going to answer it. Some tried from time to time, knocking on the door, then loudly proclaiming that they knew I was in there—I was, but I wouldn't answer. Well, I was talking to the class one morning when there came a frantic knocking on that back door. Everybody in the room that day knew the person on the other side of the door needed some help. So, without hesitation, I opened the door. One of my students, a beautiful girl, practically fell into my arms, crying.

"What's wrong?" I asked as I ushered her back outside to provide some privacy.

"Ms. Miller, I had sex with him and now he won't answer any of my calls," she whispered, tears streaming down her face, as she struggled to catch her breath between sobs. My heart broke for her, but the damage was already done.

Hear me and hear me well, ladies in your teens and even in your thirties and above: If a guy really likes you, not having sex with him is not going to change how he feels about you; likewise, if a guy doesn't care about you, having sex with him is not going to change that. You can't make him like you—not even with sex. You might make him want you temporarily, but sex is not going to make him care about you. All you're going to end up being is hurt. And smashed.

And another thing: Ladies, if you find yourself in a situation where you realize a guy has been stringing you and, at least, one other female along, do not take your hurt and frustration out on the other woman while allowing the guy to be completely off-the-hook. Why are you so upset with her? And why are you not that upset with him? And let me just tell you that the person you should be most upset with is YOU! Had you not been so quick to share the cookie, you would have realized you were dealing with a cookie monster. If you tell a guy that you are not going to have sex with him right away, and he bolts—chances are he was a cookie monster. And please, do not make the mistake of thinking that your cookie is the cookie to make him commit and be in a full-fledged relationship with you. Have you ever seen the cookie monster from a popular television show for children? Have you seen that little monster as he devours cookies? Go online and check him out, if you're not familiar with him. We're not talking about a cookie connoisseur, who can appreciate a cookie and WAIT for a cookie—no, we're talking about a monster, who eats as many cookies as he can get his little monster hands on, stuffing them into his mouth—cookie crumbs flying everywhere.

And gentlemen, if as you are reading this you realize you are a cookie monster and have no intentions of changing your ways, then start introducing yourself to women as such. You should say to them: "Hi, I'm [insert name], and I'm a cookie monster." Be up-front and honest about who you are and about what you do—state your objective from the beginning, letting them know that all you're interested in is sex. Stringing a woman along is not cool—stringing multiple women along is criminal. Don't toy with women's emotions.

Now, let me also address the women who have been known to run game on men—oh, yeah, they are out there. These are women who use the cookie to get men to purchase things for them. Women who make men think they like them to see what they can get out of them like a mani/pedi, or an appointment with the hair stylist on their dime. That type of manipulation is foul, and it does take place, so beware of the heartbreaking female as she is out there, too, in search of her next victim. I know good guys who have had their hearts broken by the so-called lady in their life. They can hardly get themselves together after their experiences with some of these women. As a sister to a brother, there were many times when I pulled him aside to share my concerns about some female. I believe I have a special place in my heart for men, because I have a brother. It is my opinion that men don't often get the care they need, because they're men and people act as though men don't need protecting sometimes too. They do.

Single men, it is not your responsibility to be paying for your girlfriend's hair and nails. It just isn't. Is she an able-bodied woman? Okay, then. Why are you expected to give her money when you get paid from your job? The two of you don't have any children together, so why are you giving her money? All of these transactions keep you from really getting to know a person for who they are at their core—instead, all that you have between you is the cookie and a couple bundles of weave. Lastly, married men, please, reconsider that whole *happy wife, happy life* thing, because that kind of thinking often results in some manipulative woman always getting her way in a relationship instead of there being compromise. I'm just saying.

We live in a culture that heavily pushes getting and giving the cookie—it's in the music, the advertising, the television programs, the movies, the internet, it's everywhere. All I'm saying is that once the cookie is involved, things can get cloudy—there is low visibility with all those crumbs around—making it difficult to see clearly, you know what I mean? Slow your roll... well, your cookie.

CHAPTER 6
Hello

I was running errands one day with the teenaged daughter of a friend. She noticed that as I moved about from place-to-place I said *Hello* or *Good morning* to each person with whom I came into contact. She asked in a somewhat exasperated tone, "Myndel, do you have to speak to EVERYbody?"

"Yes." I replied, smiling. "Yes, I do."

I speak to everybody. Every. Body. If you are not already in the habit of greeting people when you see them, then start doing it. When you walk into a room and there is already someone in it, it's on you to speak—say something: Good Morning! or How are you today? or Boo! Say something. And if you're speaking to someone, who looks as though they could be someone's grandpa or grandma, throw in a sir or ma'am at the end of your greeting. It's old-school, and people of that generation love it.

Here is the thing: You never know who you're going to need in this life. Speaking to people builds a bridge you may one day need to cross over. And, please, do not base whether you decide to speak on who the person is, or on the position they hold. Sometimes it is the person you would least expect that can help you. In my twenty-eight years of teaching, I cannot tell you how many times it has been a custodian who has come through for me. I have lost track of how many times it was the principal's administrative assistant who helped me out. Speak to everyone.

There have been students who came to me seeking a letter of recommendation, and I told them I would not be able to write it, simply, because they had not been in the habit of speaking to me; they weren't in the habit of saying *Good morning* to me—even after I initiated it, in some cases. Does that sound petty to you? Well, it's huge to me, because to me whether or not you speak to people says a lot about your character. If you were not acknowledging me all along, why are you suddenly acknowledging me now that you need a reference? You didn't see me standing at the classroom door each morning as you walked in? You didn't see me in the teacher's lounge eating lunch when you walked in? Oh, okay... keep on not seeing me, then, and get somebody else to write that letter of recommendation while you're at it. You should have been saying hello to me on a regular basis, simply because it was the right thing to do. The old-school generation calls it good home-training. We need to get back to speaking to people, because I know big, hard-back individuals, as my Trinidadian mother would say, who will look you in your face as you are speaking to them and still say nothing.

Know that not everyone is going to respond when you greet them, but that's okay—just smile and keep on saying hello. The world needs it.

CHAPTER 7
Use Money—Don't Worship It.

    Please tell me there are not any pictures on any of the social media platforms of you *making it rain*. What is that about anyway? You know, I often hear people misquoting the Bible in saying that money is the root of all evil. Money is not the root of all evil; in fact, what the Bible says is that money works everything, or in other words, money solves a lot of problems—and it does. For the person who lost their job, and their family is facing eviction, because of failure to pay the rent or mortgage, or for the family whose child is in the hospital and they do not have health insurance, or for the family whose home was destroyed by fire—money would be very helpful in each of those situations. There are very few things in this life that you will want or need to do that do not require money. Very few.

    So, it is a person's love, or greed, for money that the Bible says can cause a person to do all sorts of wicked things. For the love of money, folk will steal, cheat, lie, and even kill. People come up with all kinds of elaborate schemes to kill off a family member to get the money from the insurance policy they secretly took out on the other person. I have a friend who is a detective and went undercover as a hitman to catch a woman who wanted her boyfriend killed. Can you believe that?! And this was after she had already knocked off her husband! And she instructed him to also get rid of the kid, if the man's daughter happened to be there when things went down! True story, and it all boiled down to the love of money.

Here's the thing: You can be happy with money. It will afford you the opportunity to pay bills, purchase items you need and even those items you peep and decide you want. You can be happy without it. You can also be unhappy with money. Sounds crazy, right? I know what some of you are thinking: Let me experience some of that unhappiness! Please and thank you! As crazy as it sounds, though, there are people who have much money, but they're miserable. So, instead of aspiring just to be rich so that you can make it rain, aspire also to affect some positive change in your community and in our world. Don't be impressed with big houses and fancy cars and designer labels—like works of art in a museum, they can absolutely be appreciated for their beauty, but they are things to be used and yes, enjoyed, but not loved. Money is a tool that can be used to buy your necessities, and it can be used to buy your wants in this life. It is a tool to be used. Don't let the pursuit of money consume you. Also, remember that money can be used to bring a little happiness to another person's life. Many of the greatest moments in life will be those times when you are able to help someone else; to ease their burden a little bit, or to bring a little sunshine to their day—money, used wisely, can do that.

I'll let you in on a little secret: People who really have money—I'm talking real money; not a couple thousand from a tax refund—don't usually feel the need to prove anything to anybody. People who really have money are often the humblest, most unassuming people you'd ever hope to meet. So, if you find yourself on social media holding-up a stack of ones wrapped in a hundred-dollar bill, that's a dead giveaway to the rest of us that you're only tax-refund rich.

CHAPTER 8
What Is Your Problem?

The other thing I could have been paid handsomely for was every time I asked a student what they wanted to be when they grew up. Typically, what would occur is the student would begin searching the ceiling (or the floor) for an answer. All too often the response was a shoulder shrug. It hasn't been until pretty recently that I read an article suggesting we instead ask young people *What kinds of problems do you want to help solve?* The issue with asking a young person what they want to be when they grow up is that the question can be limiting in that they will come up with what they know, which is often limited to two or three things; for example, many of the students I talk to now want to be certified nursing assistants (CNAs), which is fantastic unless the only reason they plan to pursue that career path is because their aunt is one. The disposition alone of some people should disqualify them from ever becoming a CNA—if you don't truly have a heart for people, please stay away from all healthcare facilities. I do not believe you are here on this planet to grow old working a job that you hate. I just don't believe that. Find out what you were put on this earth to do.

I used to have the following quote on one of my bulletin boards: The two most important days in a person's life—the day they are born, and the day they discover why. More important than making money is understanding your reason for getting out of bed every morning. Your purpose in life always involves providing something for others. There is at least one gift—one talent—that you have that others need. There is something that you are good at doing that benefits others and makes you feel worthwhile. It is usually connected to something you enjoy doing naturally. What is it for you? Do you enjoy organizing cluttered areas? Are you exceptionally good at drawing cartoon characters? Do you make the best tamales this side of Mexico City? Are you the one in your circle of friends that people go to for advice? Hello! Folks, those are talents that are meant to point you in the direction of your purpose in life. I, firmly, believe that you have one. Discover and fulfill your purpose. And when you have an idea of what your purpose is, go after it. Let nothing and no one—yourself included—stop you.

The one thing we don't lack in this world of flawed beings is problems, so which ones do you want to help solve? Do you want to help people whose cars don't work? Do you want to help people design the house of their dreams? Do you want to help solve the homelessness issue in our country? Do you want to help bring an end to human trafficking in your area? What you don't want is to get to the end of your life, wishing you'd fulfilled your purpose.

The other thing I would like to submit for your consideration is that you always keep yourself open to possibilities that you simply had not considered before. Case in point: I now co-host a podcast with two of my colleagues who also happen to be my friends. I didn't even really know what a podcast was until one friend approached me and the other friend about doing one. Hosting a podcast was not what I considered to be in the realm of possibility for me. Never in a million years would I have predicted doing something like this. And the real kicker is that I'm the one who edits and uploads each episode to the platform for streaming. Me! The lady who was content with the flip phone (more on that later). Be open to the possibility that you don't know all there is to know about who you are and what you have to offer the world. And then, get out of the mindset that whispers to you that your age somehow means you're unable to accomplish certain things. I told you, I'm fifty-one and still discovering things about who I am and what I'm capable of doing. Am I too old to host a podcast? Am I too old to write books? Apparently, not—neither are you too old, or too young.

    Okay, can we agree on the fact that you did not create yourself? It's not like you woke up one morning and sketched out a drawing of your body and then went about gathering the materials to put yourself together. And if that it is what happened with you, then we need to talk 'cause I am now your agent, and we're about to hit the talk show circuit. You did not make yourself. Can we agree on that? Okay, cool. Now, because you did not create yourself, isn't it possible that you don't know everything there is to know about you? Isn't it, then, possible that there are some talents and some gifts inside of you that you are not yet aware of? I believe there are, so be open to trying new things, and going to new places, and talking to new people. Do not limit yourself to that little bit you know about yourself. Do not allow others to limit you either with what they feel they know about you. Again, and most of all, do not limit yourself. Some of us say far worse things to ourselves than anyone else has ever said to us. I will be honest and admit that I am my biggest critic. I often need to remind myself to do what I am saying to you: Don't limit yourself—stay open to the possibilities that are you.

CHAPTER 9
Get Smart

Years ago, I allowed a group of students to persuade me into making the switch from a flip phone to a so-called smart phone. My flip phone's name was Phillip and he fit snugly into the palm of my hand, and his little screen seemed to be unbreakable—probably due to the fact that it was not a touch screen, unlike these new-fangled phones with screens that must crack if you look at them too hard, judging from how many messed-up screens I've noticed. Technology is a pretty wonderful thing, I must admit. A word of advice, though: When you're supposed to be carrying on a conversation with someone, refrain from frequent checking of your phone. It's rude, particularly to older adults, who can recall a world without cellphones.

If you are not careful, you're going to waste your life away on your electronic devices. You'll miss out on the moments that really matter. If you are not careful, you're going to look up one day and realize five years of your life have passed you by. You'll realize that instead of working on your own life, you've been sitting idly by as others lived their lives. These phones and the internet can be very addictive. I used to tell my students they acted like crackheads when it came to your phones—they behaved as though they couldn't live without them. I'm pretty sure some needed rehab. I, truly, believe that in the next few years, there really will be a need for cell phone addiction rehabilitation centers; in the meantime, practice going for extended periods of time without your phone and without accessing the internet. Spend some time during each day in quiet where you're not being bombarded with the voices of others—learn to be alone with your own thoughts sometimes. Read a book for goodness' sake. Play some Words with Friends with your actual friends—these may or may not be the same as your social media friends. Be careful, because the way some of you are behaving with these devices is not so smart. I don't know how many of us realize that these platforms and electronic games and devices were created to be addictive. The intention was to create a device that people would become addicted to—I find that interesting and more than disturbing. Be smarter than your phone.

CHAPTER 10
N*gga

At the beginning of each school year—probably the first day of school, now that I think about it—I explained to each of my classes that **I didn't want to hear the n-word**. I told them that I didn't want to hear it from people who looked like me, and that I sure didn't wish to hear it from those who didn't. Here's what I'd like for you to consider as you move forward in your adult lives: Don't use it at all.

There is a long history of hatred attached to that name. Some will tell you the fact that it is used, now, as a term of endearment has taken the destructive power out of the word. I disagree. The intention of this word was to tear down, and I believe that that's what it continues to do. There have been a couple of instances in my high school teaching career when I've heard a white student use the word, and I've shut it down immediately. In both instances, the white student used it while conversing with black students. I guess they were friends. I, too, converse with white people on an almost-daily basis, but I have yet to know one, who could use the n-word in my presence and not hear from me. I have yet to meet the white person—and I know some cool white people—who is that cool with me.

But there is nothing as disheartening as those times when I've heard black students refer to each other using that word. I would shut it down, then, too—especially, then. I don't like to hear black women refer to black men in that manner. Really, black woman? He must hear it from you, too? There are so many other, better words that we can use to address each other. We are such a beautiful, strong, and brilliant people—we can do better. Come on, let's do better.

CHAPTER 11
Learn How to (and not to) Give to Others

Giving freely and willingly from the heart is one of the greatest feelings in the world. Life shouldn't just be about getting. What have you done for someone else lately? No strings attached—no bringing it up at some later date when they don't do what you want them to do. Give because you want to—not because you're looking for praise or some sort of favor in return for your giving. And when you give, you don't need to go blabbing it to everybody—posting it on social media platforms far and wide.

It's also imperative that you learn how not to give. Don't give because someone is pressuring you to give—trying to make you feel badly (guilty) about not giving to them. It's called manipulation and it's wrong. It's wrong if your mother does it, it's wrong if your sister does it, it's wrong if your so-called friend does it. Beware of people who, instead of getting a job, are always ready to share a sad story about why they need to borrow some money. That sad story, which is sometimes accompanied by tears, is a form of manipulation—don't fall for it. I've made that mistake. I don't make it anymore.

Many years ago, to pay-off debt, I took on a rather large paper route, in addition to teaching full-time at a local elementary school. In the wee hours of the morning, I would deliver newspapers, then go home to shower and dress before going to teach my fourth graders. I delivered those papers seven days a week—rain or shine—for two years to accomplish my goal. When you've worked hard and made sacrifices in your own life, it's perfectly okay to expect the same of others before you decide if and how to help them. You will find that there are people who genuinely need help—they are doing all they can in their own might, and simply need a hand. You will also find those who are all about getting what they can from you, with the least amount of work and sacrifice on their part. It's up to you to pay attention, and to discern the difference. Learn how not to be a foolish giver—of your money, or of your time.

CHAPTER 12
Cars in Cash

I can recall going with my parents for a test drive, many years ago in Tampa, when the sales guy said, "Well, you know, a car payment is just one of those things you'll just always have." I didn't say anything back then—I was a kid in the backseat of the car, and he wasn't talking to me—but I can recall wondering *Why? Why does that have to be the case?* I'm here to tell you it does not have to be the case—**you can pay cash for a brand-new vehicle**. I realize that if you are just starting out financially, there is a good chance you're not exactly rolling in the dough—I remember what it was like just starting out. I share these thoughts with you in the hopes that seeds will be planted in your hearts and minds, so you'll know that your story doesn't have to look like everybody else's story. You can manage your money in such a way that you can buy a car (and a house, too) outright—no financing (borrowing money from the bank). When it comes to cars, it is important to note that they depreciate in value, so keep that in mind before you go getting yourself into car-payment debt. That new-car smell can be quite intoxicating. Make sure when you visit the car dealership that you're not committing a BUI and buying under the influence.

On May 15, 2005—I can tell you the exact date, because I've kept a journal since high school—I saw a picture of a H3 in a magazine and when I saw it, I wanted it. An off-road vehicle was not a vehicle I had ever pictured myself in, but for whatever the reason, this vehicle appealed to me. At the time, I was driving a previously-owned little car that I had paid $500 cash for—the car was old, but well cared for—and the air conditioning used to give out, requiring me to take it to a mechanic for freon. If you've never been to Florida, you may not be able to appreciate how unbearable the heat can feel without AC. It can be brutal. I took the page with the ad out of the magazine and kept it on my desk at home. This next part sounds a little crazy, but do you promise not to laugh at me? Okay. When I began spotting the H3 around town, I would say *Humma, humma, humma*, and smile to myself as if to say to the vehicle *I'm coming for you*. Hey, you said you wouldn't laugh!

In the Fall, I was teaching fifth graders, and in talking to them one day I shared that that would be my next vehicle. I felt safe in sharing it with them. What I don't recall sharing with them, but I will share with you is the fact that I didn't want a car payment—I wanted to just buy the car outright. Cold, hard cash—well, cold hard cashier's check. Later in that school year, one of my students, a little boy whose nickname was Pinky, brought me a tiny toy H3 that I have to this day. Children believe in possibilities, don't they? We need to be more like them in that respect. I opened an account to start saving money toward my purchase. Time kept on passing as it is known to do. On a leisurely stroll at a local shopping area, I found myself in a toy store of all places where my eyes fell on a black H3 ten times bigger than the gift from Pinky, with a sunroof, and driver and passenger-side doors that opened. You know I had to buy it, right? It went on my desk at home next to the first one. That school year ended.

I was sitting at that same desk on the twelfth of September, in the new school year, reading a newspaper when I noticed the house next door was on the market for over $250,000, and the thought of selling my own home came to mind. The house I lived in, then, was the third I'd purchased, so I was already of the mindset that houses were property to be bought and sold. Buying a 'forever' home which people talk a lot about now has not been a desire for me—at least, not yet. The fact that the economy favored the seller made the sale a no-brainer for me; actually, the housing market at the time more than favored the seller; things were kind of crazy in that sellers were pretty much just naming their prices, and buyers would just scoop up the properties. I listed the house twelve days later, and it closed at the end of December. The sale allowed for the pay-off of student loans, and the purchase of—you already know. When my possession of the vehicle was imminent, I rented one for a weekend just to make sure it was indeed what I wanted. I went to the grocery store, and I drove to a friend's the next town over—that was some smooth driving. Not having payments was even smoother.

One of the morals of the story is this: Decide on what you want. Keep that mental (or physical) picture of it at the forefront of your thoughts. You will find ways to make it happen. Your story can be unlike anyone else you know. Just because no one in your family has done it, doesn't mean it can't be done.

CHAPTER 13
More Books, Less Boobs and Butt

When You Decide to Have Children—Read to Them A LOT.

Many of my students would never have imagined becoming lost in a book, but many of them have over the years. After the allotted fifteen minutes of sustained silent reading was up, I would have to repeatedly tell students to, please, put away their books for the day's lesson to begin. It was an awesome problem to have! As a teacher, sustained silent reading of books my students chose to read was the hill I was willing to die on. Books for my classroom were what I spent money on, and time each day for independent reading was nonnegotiable in my classroom. I didn't care what new initiatives and programs came down the pike, my ultimate goal as a Reading teacher was for my students to discover the joy of books and of reading. I chose to look way past a standardized test and a school grade to the parents and members of society my students would one day become.

Plenty of research out there tells us that a child who doesn't read much will likely end up not reading well; and not reading well, will likely result in not doing as well in school. Not doing well in school can lead to not being as successful in the world of work as an adult. The ability to read, and to read well is huge, so let your child see you reading, and give him/her access to many wonderful books and magazines. As you well know, there isn't much time in school that's devoted to reading for pleasure—it's sad, but true—so a love for reading will need to be fostered by you at home. It will be imperative that they see you reading, too. Lead by example. Do your child a favor and introduce them to the world of books.

Less Is More in Most Cases.

Ladies, if what you're about to put on can earn you the Employee of the Month at the strip club, then don't wear it to school. So began my spiel at the beginning of each school year regarding dress code. Students always laughed because students always knew exactly what type of attire I was talking about. Yeah, well, the same applies for the workplace. Your co-workers don't need to see your breasts, nor do they need to know the type and color of your underwear. Not too tight, not too short, not too revealing at work when it comes to clothing. You want to be taken seriously and treated professionally at work.

Oh, my goodness, gentlemen—please, stop waddling around with your boxers exposed. And I heard if you wore a belt, you wouldn't need to keep pulling up your pants or holding them up when you walk around, sir. You need to be taken seriously at work, too. The less we see of your undergarments, the better.

CHAPTER 14
Never, Never, Never Give Up

I'm pretty sure it was Winston Churchill who said that. He had, no doubt, gone through a time of struggle, and made it to the other side. That's why he was able to encourage the rest of us to keep going when the going gets tough. Life can be hard, but some of you already know that. You've experienced tough times with your family—some of you have dealt with the death of a parent; the pain of living with a drug-addicted family member, or you have a loved one who's incarcerated. Life will knock you down with what sometimes feels like a kick in the chest, and then dare you to get back up. That's exactly what I want for you to do, though—get back up. It won't be easy, and you'll feel like giving up, but don't give up. Get up, dust yourself off, and keep going. Cry, if you need to; scream, and even take a little time-out if needed, but keep going. There's a strength that comes in the going. I know what I'm talking about. I know what it is to be given a diagnosis from a doctor that knocks the wind out of you.

There have been two moments in my life that were especially dark days for me, and twice I considered the thought of just not continuing on, because surely that would have relieved the pain and despair I was experiencing. The first time I considered the thought, it was merely a fleeting thought; the second time, I entertained the thought far longer than I should have. But the idea of my parents having to deal with the aftermath of a decision like that, gave me the strength to banish the thought and to go on.

Do you know how many beautiful moments I have experienced since then? How many fantastic people have come into and added to my life, and me to theirs since then? Imagine how many more moments there are yet to be experienced and to be shared. Don't give up. Sadness and depression and anxiety and anger and feelings of abandonment and of betrayal are not emotions most people want to discuss, or admit to feeling—especially, among certain groups of people and within certain communities—but it's important to be able to discuss them and to learn how to address them and to release them. It may mean seeking the professional help of a counselor even—something that is more than okay for men as much as it is for women, and for people of color, too. Do not suffer in silence.

Over the years, what I have noticed about my students who play some type of sport was that, for the most part, these were students who knew how to lose and keep going. They knew what it was to be knocked down, and to get back up to fight another day. They reflect on the game and their performance; they make the necessary adjustments and begin preparing for the next game. Disappointments will come. Heartache and pain and loss will come. Your life will take turns that you didn't anticipate, but do not give up. People will hurt you. You're going to mess up, but don't give up. There is life after a failure. There is life after you make a mistake. There is life after someone breaks your heart. And know that as bad as things may seem at the time, it will get better. Don't give up. The sun will shine again. Have you ever been on the interstate during a torrential downpour? You have both hands gripping the steering wheel, the windshield wipers are operating at the highest possible speed; visibility is practically nil, and it is downright scary. But that rain doesn't last forever. If you keep driving, or if you pull off on the shoulder of the road to wait, the rain will eventually cease. Please hear my heart on this one: Never, never, never give up.

CHAPTER 15
Mission Control

What Is This with the Middle Finger in Pictures?

I've noticed it in many social media posts. I certainly hope that none of my students are engaging in this new trend—sadly, I'm pretty certain that some are. And what does it even mean? People, you do know that prospective employers and college admissions officers check Facebook photos to find out more about you, right? It would be a shame for your middle finger to keep the rest of you from acceptance to a university, or to keep you from a position with a company. It would be a crying shame.

Keep Your Hands to Yourselves.

It's always interesting for me to hear what students believe is okay behavior, because oftentimes it is SO very different from what I deem appropriate and right. Case in point: Is it ever okay for a man to hit a woman? I was amazed—and not in a good way—by the number of my students, who believe there is nothing wrong with it. Some tried to explain to me that sometimes the situation calls for it. Listen to me. If you are in a relationship with someone you feel needs to be smacked around from time-to-time, you are in the wrong relationship, or you need some sort of counseling, or both.

Most women often find themselves attracted to men like their fathers. That has definitely been true for me. The men I've dated have been kind, bright, articulate gentlemen, who treated me like a lady. Now, let me add that I carried myself like a lady, too. I have not been man-handled or cursed-out by boyfriends. I did not see my mother being treated in that manner by my father, so the whole notion that a man would hit me or call me something other than my name, or a term of endearment, was foreign to me.

Perhaps, you didn't grow up with a father in your home, or even in your life; maybe you did, but he was abusive… here's what I want you to know: You deserve to be treated like the special young woman that you are. You deserve to be spoken to with kindness and respect. You deserve to have doors opened for you, and chairs pulled out for you when you're out to eat. You deserve to be liked by a guy, who only has eyes for you. You deserve to be encouraged to be all that you can be in this world. You deserve to be complimented and not degraded.

And ladies, as the sister of a brother, I also don't condone a woman putting her hands on a man. I've seen young women reach out to slap a young man's face, or punch him in the arm, and it's wrong; and I call out to them and tell them it's wrong and why. I'm preaching to my male students about not hitting women, then here you come looking like you're vying for mixed martial artist welterweight champion—STOP IT. Keep your hands to yourselves.

Being struck by the man or woman you're in a relationship with is not normal behavior. You're not supposed to know what that feels like—it's not supposed to be your norm. Know your worth. It saddens me to see bright, beautiful young women settle for less than they deserve. He shouldn't call you derogatory names. That's never funny. By the way, if you laugh it off, then that's license for him to say it again. And again. And again. We teach people how to treat us. We do. When we let things slide—a derogatory name, him smushing you in your face with his hand, a back-hand, a shove—we are co-signing the behavior. Know your worth. Don't be his punching bag. Don't be his booty call. If he acts brand-new when the two of you are around other people, and he is only interested in spending time with you privately—lose him. A decent young man will acknowledge you in the wide open—in the presence of his friends. A decent guy will acknowledge you in the presence of other females—you won't have to be concerned with him trying to get with every Tina, Deena, and Harriet. Know your worth. You deserve to be treated respectfully and handled with care. Start by treating yourself respectfully and with care.

The Only Person You Can Control Is You.

Trust me when I tell you that the sooner you learn this one, the better off you will be. It will save you undue stress. No matter how much you love a person and wish for them to make better decisions, they will have to want better for themselves. I'm mostly thinking about people you love, who are involved in self-destructive behaviors like drug and alcohol abuse, or might be in abusive relationships, but this lesson isn't limited only to those situations.

It hurts to witness a loved one's struggle or downward spiral—I know; I've been there. I had allowed myself to become almost sick with worry—hair falling out—until it hit me one day that while I was worrying, my loved one was living what he considered to be his best life. As sad and destructive a life as I thought it was, he was livin' it, honey, while I'd placed my life on hold, in a way. I had to learn to distance myself from the whole situation. I had to stop allowing the subject of that certain loved one to dominate my conversations and my thoughts—in essence, I had to get a life apart from him. Still loved him, but I could no longer be consumed with details of the circumstances surrounding him and his choices. Notice that I said, I had allowed myself? Yep. It was a choice I had made, and as soon as I saw the error of my ways, I made a different choice—a healthier choice for me. Because at day's end, I am the only person whose actions I can control. You are the only person whose actions you can control. You got that?

We all have choices to make in this life. Those choices will determine the quality of life we will have. You can't control anybody else—you can control how you respond to other people's actions. But that's it.

CHAPTER 16
Gratitude and Gutter Greetings

Be Grateful.

Don't ever lose that. Showing appreciation is what makes people want to continue giving to you and looking out for you. Be grateful even for the smallest kindness, because the reality is that people don't have to do a doggone thing for you—nobody owes you anything. Do you hear me? Not one solitary thing. You are entitled to zilch, nothing, nada, nuttin', zero. So, when someone does do something for you—anything for you—be appreciative, because they are under no obligation to do it.

Teach your children and grandchildren how to be grateful. Once they've started making attempts to talk, these lessons in gratitude can begin. For example, as you're handing them the sippy cup, tell them, "Say 'thank you.'" Don't release the sippy cup until they release a 'thank you.' The same thing goes for the word 'please'. I grew up hearing my mother repeat what she'd heard her mother say: You don't raise your children only for you. In other words, if you allow (and even encourage, in some instances) your children to develop bad habits when it comes to their behavior, then you're making it difficult for them to receive the help they will undoubtedly need in life. We all need other people to help us on this journey. Practice showing gratitude for the kindnesses of others. Gratitude breeds kindness.

B*tches, Miss Me with That.

When did *Hey, B*tch* become an acceptable greeting for a friend? I missed that memo. Ladies, when did it become okay to greet anyone like that—much less someone you consider a friend? She's a really low-class woman who will refer to another woman as a b*tch. Low-class—I don't care who she is, or what she does and how successful she may be at doing it—she's low- to no-class. There's something wrong with that; it's not the type of behavior you should want to emulate. That's not the type of language you should use—not even in jest. It's vulgar and crude and you're better than that, and so are your sisters—your fellow female beings. Life can be hard enough as a woman in this world, without having to hear such vulgarity from someone who is supposed to have empathy for your struggles.

And you can already guess where I stand when it comes to young men, who refer to young women as b*tches and hoes and thots. You don't have the time of day for a guy, who doesn't know how to properly address you. Here's the thing though: People know who to say what to. You teach people how to treat you. You saying nothing is the same as your giving them permission to do it. I guess I'm just kind of weird like that, because what you're not going to do is call me a b*tch and I smile back at you like all is well—not to my face you're not. Oh, no.

And speaking of *not to my face*, can we stop talking about each other behind each other's backs? Women are probably the absolute worst when it comes to this. We need to stop it though, because the only thing it gets us is worked up in most cases. Stop engaging in conversations where disparaging comments are being made about others—even if the comments are true—because you're better than that. Have you ever heard the saying: Small minds discuss people, average minds discuss events, great minds discuss ideas? If we put as much thought into marketable ideas as we do into gossipin' an' cussin', some of us would be multi-millionaires by now. Yeah, I said it.

CHAPTER 17
Dark and Different

Beautiful, Dark-skinned People.

I was known by students and colleagues alike for having a picture of a well-known handsome, dark-skinned actor displayed in my classroom, so my love for dark chocolate men is no secret. In fact, one of the most handsome men I have ever seen was a young man on the University of Florida campus. I was walking past Yon Hall one day during my freshman year, I believe, when I noticed this guy walking toward me with the darkest skin my eyes had known at that point in my life, and it (and he) was so beautiful to me.

My father is a dark-skinned man. I grew up in a home where dark skin just was—there were no derogatory comments, no apologies for not having a lighter complexion. I understood that being beautiful and having a dark complexion were not mutually exclusive.

I shudder when I hear black people say of dark-skinned blacks or Hispanics and Latinos, he (or she) is *so black* as though that's a bad thing. It also saddens me to hear a dark-skinned black person put himself down, because of his complexion. I used to think that only black people did this, but I have since witnessed Hispanics and Latinos do it too—this is a belief among many all over the world, I am certain.

By the time this book is published, I would have already published my first children's book whose main character is, intentionally, a dark-skinned sixth grader named Peter. The second children's book that will follow soon after will also feature a dark-skinned male child, because I intend to do all I can to help change this narrative. Children of color, in general, need to see images that resemble them in books; dark-skinned boys and girls especially need to see these beautiful images gracing covers.

Beautiful, dark-skinned people don't believe the lie that continues to be perpetuated in this world of ours—that dark skin is somehow inferior and ugly. And don't you help to perpetuate it in the way you talk about yourself, or in the way you talk to your children. And while I'm at it, please stop with the *she's pretty for a Black girl*, too. I usually address these ignorant statements when I hear them, because you need to be reminded of your wonderfulness, and the ignorant and hateful people do, too. My hope is that you learn to recognize people's ignorance and their own self-hatred, and learn to love your beautiful, dark chocolate selves.

A Different World.

Do you want a different life from some of the ones you've grown up around? You can have it. It's okay to want something different. You should want more; you should desire greater. It's okay to want to move out of your neighborhood, or to leave your hometown—never to return. It's okay to desire the finer things in life, because it's a whole different kind of stay at a five-star hotel than it is at a motel with no rating. Whole different experience—thread count is real, folks. Now, this may seem like a paradox—it's not—but at the same time that I encourage you to desire bigger and better and more, I also want you to stop thinking that more always has to mean money. It doesn't. More, for you, might mean a peaceful environment, because your home life was one wrought with chaos and arguing. Bigger might mean a home where the cupboards always have food, and the bills are paid on time. When I was a teenager, I can remember beginning to look at my parents' lives and deciding which of their ways I wanted to continue in my own life as well as what I never wanted to repeat when I was on my own. You're supposed to do that!

    Don't let someone else's life dictate to you what you can and cannot achieve in yours. No. Their story doesn't have to be your story. Now, be prepared to go after it—and in some cases, to fight for it—but it can absolutely be yours. And don't allow others to make you feel badly about wanting more or something different out of life. There are miserable, hating people in this life, who will try to make you feel badly about wanting to better yourself; they'll accuse you of being a sell-out, or of acting like you all that, or of being bougie. To use common vernacular: Chile, please. Let them talk with their small minds. Let them talk. Pursue your dreams despite what others may say about you. That's that hate talking, and you don't have time to listen to it. You also don't have time to share your dreams with haters. When you recognize that someone is a hater, stop telling them your business and your next move. Beware: Sometimes the haters are in your own family. Pursue your dreams despite what you may some days say to yourself, because sometimes we can be our own worst enemy. Take the time to dream dreams, and then pursue them.

CHAPTER 18
Harvest Time

You Reap What You Sow.

So, as much as possible, sow good seed; respectful seed, kind seed, honest seed. Many times, people will do their dirt, thinking that because nothing happened right away, then nothing's going to happen—not so. You see, a farmer will tell you the thing about sowing a seed is that the plant or the harvest doesn't come right away. It takes a minute, and by a minute I mean a while. Yeah, enough time for a person to think that nothing is going to come of it. Some of you haven't lived long enough yet to know the truth of this statement, but I've been around long enough to see people (and sometimes their children) have to deal with the consequences of them sowing messed-up seed.

My Mom shared a story with me once about a lady who used to make fun of her friend who walked with a limp. Some friend, huh? But she did—behind her friend's back, she used to mock the way she walked. Fast forward some years, and the ridiculing friend had gone on to have a daughter who went on to have some issues with her feet and ended up walking with—you guessed it. Was that just a coincidence? And, so it is in my very humble opinion, that I suggest to people who have children or who plan to have children, that they be even more careful of how they treat others 'cause their seed may adversely affect their seed. You feel me? The same principle, also, applies when you sow good seed, know that it may take a while for you to see the fruit of it. Even though it's taking a while to reap the benefits, know that it's coming. Don't stop doing what's right. Your perseverance and work will pay off, but be careful because your laziness will, too.

Do the Right Thing.

Get into the habit of doing what is right, especially when no one is looking—that's how character and integrity are developed. Treat that elderly patient of yours with care and respect—not just because it's your job, but because they are a fellow human being and should be treated humanely; come to a complete stop at that stop sign, even though there isn't a soul around. Speak up for that classmate or colleague, who seems to be having a hard time speaking up for themselves. Don't do what's right so that you can be seen by others—wrong motives are eventually exposed. Do what's right, because it's right. By doing the right thing, you can become a change agent for making your community a better place—the world could use a little more of that.

This is the Only Body You Get—Take Care of It.

Whether it's walking, or running, (I am amazed at people who run when no one is chasing them!) or cycling, or swimming (yeah, not doing this one either)—get active and stay active.

A few years ago, I started working out with a personal trainer. I know that not everyone can afford one—there was a time when I couldn't either, but now I can. I tried the whole gym membership thing, but I've found—after spending money on DVDs and home gym equipment and cute workout attire—that I need another person to be accountable to when it comes to exercising. I've also found that, for me, if that other person is an attractive man it's MUCH easier for me to be accountable. You feel me? My plan is to develop the habit of exercising, getting to the place where I'm disciplined enough to work out on my own. I used to say I was disciplined in several areas, but that physical fitness was not one of those. I am working toward changing that narrative.

And here's another thing—a crazy thing: Why do people think that slim people don't need to exercise? EVERYBODY needs some form of exercise! #slimpeopleneedittoo When my peers hear that I work out, their response is always one of surprise, but why? Come on, people. Now, I'm not counting calories and I don't own a scale—I'm not doing all that; people can drive themselves to the point of insanity with that and I refuse. I very seldom drink sodas. I do pay attention to the amounts of sugar and sodium on labels. I eat whole-grain pastas and brown rice; leafy, green vegetables; salmon. What's pretty cool is that when you develop healthier eating habits, you actually develop a taste for healthier foods; that becomes the taste that satisfies you more than the junkier foods.

Do I still treat myself to a thick, juicy burger with raw onions, tomato, mayo, ketchup, and mustard? Absolutely! On Fridays, I eat take-out from somewhere—most of the time, it's some type of chicken or pasta dish with vegetables, but sometimes it's not. French fries call my name, too—sometimes I answer.

The other thing we don't pay enough attention to, is the importance of getting proper rest. Not getting enough sleep at nights has actually been shown to take years off of your life—literally. Do your body a favor and establish a bedtime and do your best to stick to it. Oh, my goodness, I know it can be hard! I struggle with it myself. And while there will be times when you may have to put in a little overtime to work on your own project, staying up late 'cause you're scrolling some social media site is probably not the best use of what should be your sleep time. I do know that one of the ways to help is to put the phone down.

If you are a person of color, you need to pay particular attention to your health. One of the things the recent pandemic has brought to the forefront is the fact that blacks and other people of color in the United States are disproportionately affected by the coronavirus disease. But even long before this outbreak, our communities had higher rates of other diseases like diabetes and high blood pressure. The reasons for this are varied, but if we do all that is in our power to do—such as eating way more fruits and vegetables, less fried foods, way less sodas, and get to moving—we can make a difference for ourselves and for future generations.

Just Chill.

The older you get, the more you realize that very few things REALLY matter. Doing what you were put on this earth to do, matters. Spending time with the people in your life, who love you unconditionally, and who you love in return, matters. Getting all worked-up over something ignorant somebody said or posted? Please. So not worth your energy, or your peace of mind.

CHAPTER 19
House, Sweet House

In the original version of this book, I mention trap houses, because that was something some of my seniors and I joked about throughout that particular school year. During any school year, students and teachers alike can grow a bit weary and consider throwing in the towel; those thoughts can come more frequently and more forcefully, when you're a student in your last year of high school. During moments of frustration, there were a few students, who would blurt out, *Hey, Ms., I'm just gonna quit school and get a trap house.* I would give the student a side eye, other students would laugh, and class would continue.

Here's what I do want to say concerning houses: Get one. Homeownership is for more of you than you realize. There is a lot of talk now about having more than one stream of income. Homeownership can lead to you having additional income and resources at your disposal. Some of you are not interested in buying a house at all, and that's cool. Some of you will want to own one house—the house of your dreams—and make it your forever home, which is also a beautiful thing. And then, there are some of you who won't be interested in living in the same house for the rest of your life, but rather will prefer to buy a house and use that house to make other things happen for you.

If you purchase a house for less than it is worth, you have

what's called equity. The equity in a house can be used (for a price, of course, known as an interest rate) to help you in purchasing another house. When you purchase the second house, one of the two properties can become a rental property. Owning rental property is also known as having passive income, which means that you are making money that you don't have to actively work on much of the time. I used to share with students that while I was with them and being paid by the school district, I was also making money in two other parts of town, because I had tenants who gave me rent each month. You can also purchase a house that needs work, especially, if you know reputable, dependable people who can do the work, and then turn around and sell the house for a relatively quick profit—that's called 'flipping' a house. About a year ago, I came across an article about seven long-time friends in China, who put their money together to purchase a dilapidated mansion. They completely renovated it, and plan to live out the rest of their days in that house. Pull up the article and see it for yourself. I strongly recommend you do your homework on homeownership—use the internet, which can be so helpful in providing information on how to do practically everything, talk to others who do it, take a class. It will require you that you have decent credit, which means you need to establish the habit of paying bills on time. Are there risks involved in owning rental property? Yes, ma'am and sir. There can also be great reward.

    I should also mention that people of color can face some challenges when it comes to homeownership, which has historically been and is currently the case, for many, but it is possible. I am not oblivious to the challenges that exist for black and brown people when it comes to ownership, but because I know the benefits of owning a home, I will keep sharing it in the hopes that a seed will be planted causing you to seek out ways to make it happen. Consider those Chinese friends. I have a friend whose mother wanted to buy new cars for her two, adult grandsons. She must have spent a good twenty thousand dollars, at least, on each vehicle. What a kind and generous gesture from a woman who is not what anyone would describe as rich—not by any stretch of the imagination. She has worked hard over the years to care for her now grown children, and still goes to work each day. She happens to be a black grandmother, so it probably comes as no surprise to you that her two grandsons are black males—one of whom lives with her. Both of these young men are a part of that group I mentioned a minute ago that has historically met with challenges when it comes to owning houses, which is how you create and sustain wealth.

Look, it was her money, her choice to spend it in any way she saw fit, and it's her business, but I can't help but wonder what their lives would look like, if a different choice had been made. Homeownership is one of the ways in which you can begin to build wealth for you and for your family. Don't get me wrong. Cars are nice, but a car can't buy you a house; the equity in a house, however, can buy you a car. So, listen, if a generous family member wants to help you by buying you a car—we, now, know it can happen—seriously consider making it a down payment on a home which, I believe, can take you further financially speaking than the new set of wheels.

CHAPTER 20
Moms, Dads and Other Grown Folk

Bad Dads and Mediocre Moms

I can recall speaking to a student who referred to his estranged father as a deadbeat. I shared with him that most parents are doing the best they can with what they have, and some just didn't have much in the way of good parental examples. Some people didn't grow up in a loving family, which makes it tough. It's difficult to emulate what you've not seen or experienced.

Being a parent can't be an easy job, especially since little people don't come with a manual. Granted, there are some cases in which people have children and refuse to take responsibility for them, because they care more about themselves than they do the children; unfortunately, that does happen and it's one of those things in life that none of us controls. We don't get to pick our families—it is what it is when it comes to our parents.

Here's what we can do, though, and here is what I told this student: You can make sure that when you have a child—and let's NOT make it any time soon, teenagers—you don't repeat the ways of your father. People will disappoint you—the best-intentioned people, including parents, will disappoint you, because they're people and they are flawed. It is easier than you think to repeat the ways of your parents, which may make it necessary for you to sit down with a trained professional for counseling on how to process your feelings about your parents, identify areas of your life in which you are repeating dysfunctional ways, and develop healthier habits.

Being Grown.

Be a man or woman of your word. If you say you're going to do something—do it. You don't want a reputation for being unreliable. Being an adult (or, being grown as my students would often refer to it) means being responsible for your actions. Being grown means being accountable to and considerate of others. Many of you are under the impression that being grown is a license to come and go as you please without having to answer to anyone. Ha! (in my Alf voice; look him up.) I understand not wanting people in your business, and that's not what I'm suggesting. If something were to happen to you, though, it would be good for somebody else to have some idea of where you were supposed to be, or what your estimated time of return was. Not a detailed itinerary, but an idea.

As grown as I am, I still check-in with my Mom for two reasons: I, first and foremost, want to know how she's doing and that she's all right; secondly, as a single woman, I want to let someone know of my whereabouts for my own safety. What if I'm shopping at the grocery store when some strange man spots me, wants all of this adorableness for himself, and decides to kidnap me from the frozen food section? Who could blame him, right? But I digress—the point is that it would be helpful for someone to know that I was out running errands and should be back home in a couple of hours. If nightfall comes and I'm still not home, and not answering my phone, then others will know there's a problem because I've already established that I'm reliable—a woman of my word. If you live your life all willy-nilly—you can't be depended on to be where you say you'll be—then folk won't know to be concerned if you're missing, because you're never where you say you're going to be. This accountability thing really comes into play when you live with other people—be it family members, spouse and children, or roommates. It's called being considerate of others, and it's just plain smart and safe on your part.

CHAPTER 21
The Fear Factor

I've been doing things these past few years that have scared me, but in spite of the fear I've been pressing on and moving forward. I want to, first, tell you that there will be times in your life that you will need to do things that scare you—that is, if you want to live a fuller, more abundant life. Now, I'm not talking about anything crazy like bungee-jumping—I'm talking about stepping out of your comfort zone to do something that scares you almost to death, it seems. It will be important to do these scary things, because they will allow you a glimpse into what you're really capable of doing, and of who you really are on the inside. If you never push yourself, you may never realize that you can fly—not awkwardly flapping your wings either but soaring. What if you are actually capable of flying? In my classes, I enjoyed using short motivational videos to help keep them focused on their goals throughout the year. We looked at one in particular where the man talked about the importance of jumping; of taking a chance and doing the thing you've been dreaming of doing. He is so right! If you never jump—you'll never fully realize your potential.

I encourage you to push yourself to go after the opportunities that scare you. I encourage you to do things you have not done before, because you are afraid to do them. I encourage you to surround yourself with, at least, one person, who will push you to be your best you. Don't let it be that you get to the end of your life, and you're wondering what it could have been if you'd only pursued your dreams. I'm leading by example in writing more books, buying more properties, starting and cohosting a podcast, and pursuing some other goals, striving toward the incredible life I see for myself on the horizon—I'm taking that leap, that chance, that calculated risk. Who's with me?

CHAPTER 22
Processions, Prisons, and Pens

Drinking, Driving, and Dying.

During my first period class one morning, students were talking about the traffic on one of our major roads due to an accident that killed three people. Three young people. A single-car accident that was still under investigation at that time, but officials were already stating the car had been traveling at a high rate of speed. We all knew there was probably some drinking involved. Look, I don't drink alcohol—it's just not my thing. Have I ever tried it? Yep, I took a sip of a couple of things in my adult years, and that cemented for me that I wasn't missing anything. Not too long ago and out of curiosity, I asked a gentleman his reason for drinking, and he explained to me that he was on the shy side and when he's out at a club, alcohol gives him the courage to approach women and to be comfortable carrying on conversations—he said it's referred to as 'liquid courage.' Seems to me that that ain't really courage, then, but okay. To each, his own, right?

I am convinced that much of this alcohol thing is conditioning—just like with the addictive features that are intentional, well thought out components of these social media platforms, and the reason why we find it so difficult to stay away from them, even when we want to. We are being conditioned to want to drink. I have chaperoned a couple of proms since becoming a high school teacher, and I can tell you that those venues are decorated to look like clubs and the drinks, though, nonalcoholic, are made to look like those served at an establishment for the 21 and up crowd. If we are in fact being conditioned to drink, then why? And by whom? And since I'm out here wondering, why so many liquor stores in the neighborhoods with the highest number of poor, people of color? So many liquor stores and so few farmers markets. Haven't you ever wondered? Some people do drink, though, and that's their prerogative; likewise, if you choose to partake of alcoholic beverages—if you are of age, of course—that's your business. Should you decide to drink, and then get behind the wheel of a car/truck, it, then, becomes my business. Don't drink and then drive.

    During my third period class on that same day, a student asked me whether I had known a particular former student. His name did not sound familiar to me, so she proceeded to show me a picture of him, strategically placing her thumb over the inappropriate gesture he happened to be making in the photo. He looked somewhat familiar, but he definitely had not been one of my students. I asked why she was inquiring of my knowledge of him, and she proceeded to tell me that he had been killed the night before. He was shot in the parking lot of some club. She said it so matter-of-factly, too; like I'd asked her to tell me the time.

    There is a saying that I grew up hearing from my mother: Old people must die—young people may. It seems that those words are becoming truer and truer in this world. There was once a time when it was almost unheard of for young people—teenagers—to die; there were only funerals, it seemed, for old people. Now? Young people are dying at what I consider to be an alarming rate, and such violent deaths, too!

    If you choose to drink, then don't drive. If you choose to

drive, then don't text. And as much as you possibly can, don't frequent places where you know some craziness is liable to 'jump off' as you say. Just don't do it.

You Don't Have Time to Do Time (So, don't be stupid, or be with Stupid).

I had just wrapped-up my second year of teaching high school students and had just enjoyed my second graduation ceremony when I was spotted by one of my students from my first year of teaching high school. I was happy to see him—glad to know that he was doing well. Students have no idea how much good it does a teacher to know that their students have gone on to become productive members of our communities. In addition to helping students in a particular subject-area, a good life is ultimately what we want for each of you.

Days later, I would read in the local newspaper that that same student and his brother, who I'd also had as a student, were arrested for an alleged armed-robbery attempt. The younger brother ended up being shot, because the gentleman who had been their intended victim was also carrying a firearm. What in the world they were thinking, I couldn't tell you but let me say this: Don't ever be so tempted by making fast money that you risk your freedom and your life to engage in something so crazy and so wrong. Do you understand me? No amount of money is worth your freedom. But you won't get caught, right? Because you are so much smarter, right? I know, I know.

Steer clear of criminal activity and of those who you know engage in it. I have had the opportunity to visit several prisons—even a couple maximum-security prisons where they check even your scalp before you are allowed in. I have had the chance to talk to some of the youth offenders, who were kept separate from the adult population—one young man I can still remember after all this time, because he kept repeating that he just wanted to see his mother. I visited another prison and saw a former classmate from high school. I have had my own personal experience when a family member did some time in prison—in many ways, we served that time right along with him. You don't want that—not for you or for your family. No brand name sneaker is worth it. No man is that fine that you decide to see him although you know he participates in illegal activities. You do not want to find yourself in the car, or in the house when things go down. You do not have time to hand over years of your life to our penal system—nothing is worth that time.

Mary Jane, the Hookah, and Vaping.

The legalization of marijuana is happening across this country, and it provided for some interesting conversation in some of my classes a few years ago. Some of my students had alluded to the fact that this substance may have been present at some of their off-campus social events, and some had alluded to the fact that they knew people who may even have tried it a time or two. This prompted me to spend an entire class period looking at the different aspects surrounding the use of it—it will go down in my history with students as Marijuana Monday.

We read an article about celebrities who are selling marijuana-infused products—this was news to me—and making big money in what is quickly becoming a lucrative industry. We, also, looked at the physical and psychological effects of the drug; the legal consequences; the fact that this is considered a gateway drug that can lead to more serious drugs when its user begins seeking a greater high. I mentioned to students, then, that because of parents who were alcoholics or who struggled with drug addiction, some people were predisposed to addictive behaviors. Again, if

I had had my way, every single one of my students would have turned down all offers to smoke when they were out with their friends, turning up.

I get the impression that somebody wants people addicted to substances. Why else would products that are knowingly harmful be marketed more and more to younger people. Figure out why and then decide whether it's what you want. You don't have to fall for the okie doke. Whatever decision students decided to make, and whatever direction they decided to go in, I hope they went with the facts and with their eyes wide open. But these were their decisions to make, and I realized that the best I could do was present them with a little more information, so they could make more informed choices. I hope they (and you) choose wisely.

A Hookah? So, now, people are smoking out of what looks like an 'I Dream of Jeannie' bottle with a hose attached to it, and are calling it a good time? Are y'all for real? And now there's vaping, which contains the harmful drug nicotine just like regular cigarettes. Nicotine is bad news for the lungs, and the heart and for your health in general. If you have ever heard a smoker coughing and hacking, that should be enough to make you never want to put that substance into your body. That should be enough said, right? Whatever happened to good music and good food and good people being the ingredients for a good time?

CHAPTER 23
Cruising and Caring for Self

If you've never left your hometown (or the city you currently reside in) and its surrounding areas; if you've never left the state that you live in; if you've never left the United States and set foot on foreign soil—DO IT! The world is bigger than those few people you know in your neighborhood; it's bigger than that group of women down at the nail salon, or those guys that hang out on the corner, or at the barbershop.

You may not want to become a world traveler, but I feel you owe it to yourself to, at least, visit some other states—the U.S. is a beautiful country with so much to be in awe of and to experience. Once you take that first step, you may discover that you really enjoy it.

Afraid to fly? I totally understand that. No problem. Take a cruise. Start with a 3-day cruise to the Bahamas. If you book the cruise well-enough in advance, and if you travel with a buddy it can cost you as little as $300. All of your food (and there's a LOT of it) and entertainment on the ship is included in the purchase of the ticket. On the ship alone, you'll have the opportunity to meet people from all different walks of life, and of different nationalities. If you get off the ship while it's in port, you'll be able to learn about different cultures and histories—it is a truly beautiful thing. You'll begin to realize that we are all more alike than we are different. You'll realize how fortunate you are; you'll realize how much more you have to learn.

Something else I have been enjoying in the last few years is going to a nice hotel close to my house, and then checking in for a few days. I have done the same thing in nearby cities—the one stipulation, for me, is the hotel must have room service. Room service in the morning, room service at noon, and room service in the evening. I have a book, a few magazines, and there are usually a couple of good movies available on the television. Even in the case where I remain in town, it's still like getting away. It took me a little while to learn to treat myself just because, but now that I've figured it out, I'm not going back—learn early how to be good to yourself.

CHAPTER 24
Bills, Borrowing, and Being Bossed

Pay Your Bills, People.

To the very best of your ability, pay your bills on time. Will things come up every now and then that might prevent you from doing that? Yes, but make a habit of paying your bills in a timely manner. It's one of the ways for you to establish good credit, and credit is how lending institutions recognize you. A good credit score means you are a good risk for a loan, because you repay people. A bad credit score says to a lender: Alert! Alert! This booger does not pay back the people they borrow money from, and there's a pretty good chance they won't pay you back either.

Pay your bills, because it's just right. If someone provides you with a service—a place to stay, electricity, cable, a repair—they deserve to be paid for their work. Just as you like to be paid on time, other people do too. If you owe people money, don't avoid them when it comes time to pay up. Don't stop taking their calls and answering their text messages. Don't become angry with them when they ask for their money; in fact, don't make them have to ask about their money at all. Make repaying them a priority. Don't go out shopping with money you could have used to begin repaying the person. If you can only pay five dollars every time you get paid, then do it faithfully until the entire debt is eliminated. You don't get to decide how urgent it is for the lender to be repaid. Think about the urgency you felt when you were in need, and return the money with that much urgency. Pay the people!

Don't Co-Sign.

My recommendation is that you don't co-sign on a loan for anybody. I was a kid—elementary-school age—when I can recall hearing my father talk about his experience with co-signing. Apparently, he'd done that for a family member once with a car loan. That family member ended-up not making their car payments on time, and guess what? The bank was getting ready to take back their property due to lack of payment, because until you have fully paid for a car it belongs to the bank that loaned you the money to get it. Guess what else? Because my father's name was also on that loan, my father's credit was going to be affected by a default on the loan. Yeah. At that time, my Dad had his own car that was already paid for—he had no car payment—but to save his financial reputation (his credit) he took on the car payments for the car loan that the family member had neglected. Not cool, but it was an expensive lesson learned by my father. He shared the lesson with me, so that I wouldn't have to make that same mistake. I'm happy to say that his sharing was not completely in vain, because I never co-signed a loan. I would go on to make some mistakes, but not that one.

Heed the warning: Don't co-sign for a vehicle, for a lease on an apartment, for a phone… do not co-sign. Now, are there people who would actually make their payments on time, if I were to help them out by co-signing on a loan? Yep, those people do exist. Am I willing to take that chance? Nope! You will have to decide for yourself whether you are willing to take that risk. Don't be afraid to say, 'No,' and don't allow anyone to make you feel badly for saying it. And you won't owe them any explanation either, but if you feel you must say something, say, 'I don't feel comfortable doing that.'

And, hey, parents: Stop using your children's names to open lines of credit, because your credit is jacked up. There are a bunch of services available these days for people with poor credit, so fix yours and leave the little children's names and social security numbers alone.

This leads me to another nugget of wisdom my father shared with me around this same time: Don't allow someone to borrow from you, what you can't afford to lose.

Let me put it this way: If you can't afford to lose it, then don't let anybody borrow it. Every time you let another person borrow something from you, there is a chance that you will never see that thing ever again in life—be it money, your favorite book, your electric saw, your Grandma's fine china, your soccer cleats, or your car. If you can't stand the thought of losing it, don't let anyone use it.

Hey, Serial Borrowers!

If you often find yourself borrowing things from other people, then this is for you: Treat other people's things respectfully. Your goal when you borrow something from someone is to return it at the agreed-upon time in the agreed-upon condition. If you borrow an item and it becomes damaged while in your care, it is absolutely your responsibility to fix it or pay for another one. Plain and simple. There are borrowers out there, who will damage what they borrowed from you and then want to talk about how raggedy it was when they received it. The nerve. It wasn't raggedy when they needed it though—nothing was wrong with it, or with you during their time of need. I hope none of you fall into this serial borrowers' category where you're constantly needing to borrow from other people.

~~Werk~~, Work, Work, Work, Work.

Another of the many lessons I learned from my folks is the importance of a good work ethic. Both of my parents are from a Caribbean island—Trinidad, to be exact—and there used to be a running joke about the ridiculous number of jobs held by people from the islands, particularly Jamaicans. Back in the day, there was a television show that ran a sketch in which it was normal for the Jamaican characters to have as many as fifteen jobs. The sketch was hilarious, because there actually seemed to be some truth to it.

My parents believed that arriving on time to your place of employment meant being there early. This wasn't what they told me—this was what they lived in front of me; what I saw them doing from when I was a child. So, best believe that when I had my first job at a local public library, I would arrive a good twenty minutes before I was scheduled to be there. I didn't spend my employer's time tending to my own personal business either. A good work ethic means doing what needs to be done to accomplish a task—whether that requires getting up earlier, or staying later, or both. There's a certain amount of pride you take in your work, because you see your work as a reflection of you—and it is! You feel responsible for seeing the assignment through to the end. People can trust your word and depend on you.

Some of you wait until the last minute to do everything. Some of you take forever to complete tasks because you have not disciplined yourself enough to focus on the task at hand—not yet understanding that when it's time to work, it's time to work. Developing a good work ethic has made me a better person in every area of my life. It is a discipline that is necessary for good success. So, even though you may perfect it while working for someone else, you will really benefit from it when it comes time to pursue your own personal endeavors.

CHAPTER 25
Baby Mama Aspirations

Since I began teaching high school students fourteen years ago, I've heard more than a few male students talk about the prospect of having a 'baby mama'—a woman who will give birth to their child(ren), but a woman who will know at the outset of their relationship that marriage is not an option.

Me (thoroughly intrigued): So, you wouldn't even consider marrying this young lady?

A few male students: Nah, Ms. Miller, I ain't tryin' to get married.

This is the response I get when my curiosity gets the better of me as it often does when it comes to my students. 'Why not?' I usually press, only to be met with a shoulder shrug.

I find that so interesting. Here's where I believe some of that kind of thinking stems from: I believe that we as women have started settling for 'baby daddies', so now young men (some of them) are aspiring to have 'baby mamas.'

We, now, have young women who have multiple children with multiple men. When we as women lower our standards, then men (most of them) do not feel as though they need to aspire to much. I, personally, know of young women with three, four, even five children, and with almost as many different fathers as there are children. I don't know that I can adequately express how much that concerns me—and on so many different levels—but I will give it a try, because something needs to be said. Here's what we know, folks: Having sex can result in having a baby. We know this for a fact. Some of you will want to argue having protected sex versus having unprotected sex. Please, know that there are women who became pregnant after having 'protected' sex. Having sex can result in having a baby. When you have sex, there is a possibility that it will result in a pregnancy. Period. We also know that engaging in sexual activity makes you incredibly vulnerable to a slew of sexually transmitted diseases. And you should probably know that recent statistics on new cases of HIV/AIDS are not all that promising—let's not forget two of their friends named Chlamydia and Gonorrhea. Hooking-up with multiple men or women also leaves you vulnerable to a broken heart and to a lowered self-esteem. Oh, you will say you're a bad b*tch, but on the inside I know it can't feel good to find yourself in a 'baby mama' situation.

Sweethearts, not every guy is supposed to feel as though he can just holla at you—much less have easy access to the cookie! No! Get some standards! Insist that a guy approach you in a manner that is worthy of you, and that begins with you carrying yourself respectfully. For women, I, firmly, believe that the cookie is intricately attached to the heart, and therefore, it is difficult for us to share the cookie without also giving away a piece of our heart. This is why you're not supposed to be allowing cookie access to every Tom, Dick, and Harry. You are not supposed to—within a few days of meeting some guy—just plop your cookie on the table, because he told you that you're cute. No! Give that sex thing some time. Pay attention to the kinds of things a guy does, to what he says, to what others say about him. People will show you and tell you who they are, if you take the time to watch and to listen.

Gentlemen, the same goes for you. The male heart is capable of being broken, too. Listen, watch, learn and govern yourselves accordingly. If a female is exhibiting red-flag behaviors, do not ignore the flags, believing that you can somehow change her, or learn to live with her ways. One of the greatest mistakes you can make in life is to become involved with the wrong man or with the wrong woman. If there is no peace when they are around, then they are the wrong one. If they don't encourage you to be better, then they are the wrong one. Period.

CHAPTER 26
The 'tude, the Trunk, and the Inappropriate Touch

Funky, little Attitude.

There have been a few times since I started teaching at the high school level that I've encountered students with bad attitudes. I remember one young lady—and they are usually young women (what's up with that?)—who had a slick, under-her-breath rude comment for everything I said on this one particular day. This incident wasn't her first time being rude, but it was my first time addressing it with her.

I politely called her over to my desk, and quietly said to her: You have a funky, little attitude and I'm not quite sure why, but let me explain something to you. I found out a long time ago that I can't help everybody, so perhaps it is that I'm not the one to help you and that's cool, because I can see about having you placed in another class—there are others. So, you just let me know and I'll see about making that happen, okay? Great. Thanks.

I, then, smiled and walked off to help another student.

If you have a bad attitude, it's probably because you're angry or hurt about some of the goings-on in your own life. Maybe you and your Mom don't get along—you're always arguing back and forth. Maybe your Dad isn't in your life the way you'd like for him to be. Maybe between school and your job and your problems at home, you're stressed out and hating life. I understand being angry about it, but why be rude and disrespectful to people who have only been kind to you? A bad attitude will keep others from wanting to deal with you. In this world, you're going to need somebody else's help—trust me; so, don't behave in a way that's going to turn people off by sucking your teeth, snatching your head, rolling your eyes, using heavy doses of sarcasm and profanity in your interactions with others. And then, if you exhibit bad behaviors long enough, you develop a poopy reputation and people begin avoiding you like the plague. Bad attitudes can affect your ability to keep a decent job, and even to maintain healthy relationships. People do not want to deal with your foolishness. Are there good people in the world who will attempt to work with you despite your nasty attitude? Yes, there are, but keep in mind that good, well-meaning people get tired, too. In this life, you know where you've been—you don't know where you're going. Don't be in the habit of giving people your behind to kiss. You may find yourself needing the same folk to help you out.

If while you're reading this part, you find yourself sucking your teeth and/or rolling your eyes, then you are exactly the type of person I'm talking about with your funky, little attitude. Look, hear what I'm saying and change your little funky ways. If you don't hear me, life will teach you, and I don't think you want that, because life can be a tough, ruthless teacher.

What happened to the young lady I had to speak to you? Well, she never did get back to me on that schedule change, but her attitude took a 180-degree turn and she ended-up being a joy to have in class.

Junk in the Trunk.

Don't let it be that all she has is junk in the trunk. Instead of only checking the trunk, gentlemen, you need to be checking under the hood. Is it good under the hood? Is she a kind girl? Is she a smart girl? Is she angry much of the time? Does she have a bad attitude? Is she mentally unstable? 'Cause guess what? If the two of you end up not heeding my earlier warning regarding the cookie, she could end up being the mother of your child. Forever. And that DNA thing is nothing to play with.

My advice is the same for you, ladies. The minute you suspect he might be a lil' bit crazy—get out.

Several years ago, one of my colleagues introduced me to a gentleman that she thought might be a good match for me. After our initial meeting and conversation, we exchanged phone numbers. No problem. At the time, I was coaching cheerleading, and my Fridays—every single one—consisted of teaching during the day, and a football game in the evening. So, the cheerleaders and I were walking into the stadium of the opposing team, on one such Friday evening, when my cellphone rings. It's the guy, wondering what I'm up to. We were just a few days into getting to know each other—we'd had one dinner date—so I explain that we're about to go through warm-ups in preparation for the game, but I'll call later—much later. No problem. I make it through the game, then there's the trip back to school where I wait for the girls' families to pick them up. My phone rings and I explain that I'm still waiting for families to show up. I make it home. I call and talk for a bit. No problem.

The next morning, I'm running errands—pushing a shopping cart at Walmart—when my cellphone rings. Guess who? Yeah, it's the guy. He asks of my whereabouts and then offers to meet me at the Walmart. I tell him not to bother, because I'm headed toward the registers for check-out, and then I'm on my way to the next place on my to-do list. I hang-up with him, pay for my items and hop into my vehicle. I'm on my way to the next place when my phone rings. "Where are you?" is the question asked when I answer the call. "Myndel, I'm here in the parking lot at Walmart, but I don't see your vehicle." We, now, have a problem.

There is, then, a moment of silence on my end before I ask, "Why are you at Walmart when I specifically said I wouldn't be there for very long?" and he couldn't see me, but my eyebrows were good and furrowed, because I was trying to figure out why, for the life of me, he had blatantly disregarded my wishes.

I guess for some, his behavior may have come across as being sweet and caring; for me, it said that I was quite possibly dealing with a very controlling individual, who would completely disregard my feelings—not cute. I did what I am telling you to do. When I saw what I considered to be red flags, I got out. I'm sure I found a nice way to say, *It's not you—it's me.* I got out.

Far more important than a person's attractive physical features are their personality traits and their actions.

Put a Stop to the Pat.

Ladies, who wear weave—stop patting your head. It makes you look less than intelligent. Find another way to scratch your scalp, because every time you're seen doing that, if you listen closely enough you will hear doors of opportunity closing in your face. I love you and want the absolute best that life has to offer you, but seemingly small, seemingly insignificant things like this can hinder your progress. Stop it.

Can't Touch This!

I was away at college and at a hair salon getting a shampoo when the stylist—a married man and owner of the establishment—touched me inappropriately. At first, I thought his hand accidentally brushed against me, but when it happened again, I knew that he was using the towel to try to disguise the intentionality of his touch. I remember feeling a sense of shock, and then being disappointed, and later, angry, but I didn't say anything in that moment—paid him and just knew that I wouldn't return. I would later hear some women talking about him and his reputation. Then, I was well into my career as an educator, when at a social function, I leaned in to greet a married couple with what some call a 'church' hug—nothing too close—and the husband intentionally brushed his arm against me. I didn't say anything as I stood there surrounded by other people and his wife, but I did look at him with what must have been a combination of hurt and disappointment, because up to that point he was someone whose position I respected. I wish I had had the courage in those moments to open my mouth and say something to those individuals. People who are in the habit of touching others inappropriately rely on you being afraid or too shocked to say something either to them or to someone else. Say something to somebody.

I don't know a woman alive who hasn't been the subject of a cat call or two as she walks down the street, or as she stands at her car filling its tank. Or maybe has dealt with the guy who keeps looking at her chest instead of in her eyes when he talks to her. And just in case you think only women can be the subject of inappropriate behaviors, I was recently having a conversation with a gentleman who shared that a female colleague had inappropriately touched his chest under the guise of commenting on his 'working out'—he described the same surprise I had felt when I realized what was occurring on those two separate occasions. He did manage to brush her hand away, which she laughed off. His experience reminded me of an article I'd read about young boys who have been inappropriately touched by women, but the fact that they were boys the abuse—the inappropriate touch—was somehow celebrated and seen as a rite of passage instead of as the offense it was.

Unwanted touches have never been okay. Unwanted touches will never be okay. It doesn't matter that you know the person; it doesn't matter how you know the person—unwanted touches are not okay. Unwanted touches are not okay if you're a man. Unwanted touches are not okay if you're a woman. I wish I had had it in me to say something in those instances, but I didn't. Then.

CHAPTER 27
Friends, Fault-Finding, Fads, and Fathers

Show Me Your Friends, and I'll Show You Your Future.

I heard this saying somewhere along the way, and I believe there is much truth to it. The people you choose to spend significant amounts of time with, will be the people who influence your speech, how you think, and how you behave. Ever notice how after being around someone for a while, you begin using some of their phrases in your conversations? Get you—sorry, English teachers—some friends who will cheer you on to greatness.

I'm in a place now where I want to take my business endeavors to the next level, so I have intentionally sought out female entrepreneurs to learn from and to connect with. Their conversations are more along the lines of the things I think about throughout the day. They not only encourage me to strive for greater, they can provide me with actual strategies on how to go about doing it because that's what they do.

Don't be afraid to change the kind of relationship you have with certain friends, because sometimes you can be spending major time with friends who aren't really about much—you may need to spend far less time with them depending upon your life goals. Don't be afraid to seek out new friends who are doing the kinds of things you want to do. You can have different circles of friends, or acquaintances, for different interests. Birds of a feather really do flock together—are your friends eagles or buzzards? Tell the truth.

Stop Blaming Others.

Practice taking responsibility for the part you had to play in a situation. Hey, this is an area I'm working on, too. Sometimes it is another person's fault—partially—but I always look at what I could have done differently to produce a different outcome. Case in point: I place my order at the drive-through of the fast-food restaurant, pay for the meal and receive it at the window, then I continue onto my destination. When I get to where I was going, I reach into the bag and pull out what is, clearly, not my order. Am I angry with the people back at the restaurant? Yes! But guess who I'm mostly upset with? Me. Why? What could I have done? I could have looked in the bag before driving away. I am not telling you that there are not people in your life who are to blame for certain foul occurrences that took place. I'm simply suggesting that you begin looking for where and how you can do things differently. I want you to take control of the parts of your life that you're capable of being in control of—I don't want you feeling as though you're just at the mercy of others. No. Give yourself no excuses. Meet your deadlines, and when you don't—own up to it. Take responsibility for your life and its outcomes.

To hear some of you talk, it's everybody's fault but yours that your life isn't what you want it to be. Never mind the fact that you hardly come to school, and when you do come, you come late and without the necessary materials. Never mind the fact that you spend incessant amounts of time on your doggone phone, and when you're told to put it away, you say it's your mother you're communicating with as if that makes it right. And why a Mom (or Dad) would encourage their child to text them when they should be completing their assignments is beyond me and just can't be true. That can't be true, can it?

Okay, so your parents weren't the Huxtables. Whose were? (and by the way, those were fictional characters created for a television sitcom) Here's what true and real though: You are forty-two years old now and you need to let it go and move on with your life. How much longer are you going to spend blaming them? Get some counseling to help you deal with the past, if necessary, and move on. Live. Your. Life.

And another thing: Don't you ever think about the people who came before you and the price they paid so that you could have a better life than the lives they had? I do. When I think about people like Henry 'Box' Brown, and about the people who survived the Middle Passage on slave ships; when I think about little black girls who had to integrate white schools for the first time, it makes me want to be better and do better. 'Cause I don't just think about influential people of color and their legacies in February. When I think about my own parents, and the sacrifices they have made to be able to provide for me and my brother—when I think about that, I can't give myself any excuses. None. No excuses.

Pending on the Trending.

Now, here's a major life lesson for you: Just because something is popular, doesn't mean it looks good on you; for example, who knew young people would even consider walking around with gray hair?! But it was a thing—gray hair on young people was trending! Um... apparently, so was Cookie Monster-blue hair and Ronald McDonald-red hair—both looks require a special person to properly pull them off. Everybody can't. Most people can't. 99.9% of the people you and I know can't pull off those looks. Same goes for leggings, skinny jeans, and crop tops.

While I'm on the subject of clothing, ladies, let's talk undergarments for a minute. By the way, I thought that lingerie store was a secret, so how did teenage girls hear about it? Thongs and bikini-style underwear will hit you right below your tummy, and you will find—some of you are already experiencing this—that you will start developing a 'muffin top' wherein your stomach laps over your underwear, and it laps over your pants and shorts and skirts. Those low-rider jeans produce the same effect, unless you are super active and workout on the regular, or naturally have a flat stomach. Now, I am not advocating that everyone should have a six-pack, but if you are not feeling the muffin top, wearing underwear and/or pants with a higher waistline can help. I'm just saying.

Well, She's Some Guy's Daughter.

I am known, by my students, to ask the hypothetical question, because I'm always curious about their thoughts on different issues. So, I'll ask a question like 'If you find out your child is being bullied at school, how do you handle it?' or, 'If you catch your teenager crawling out of their bedroom window, what do you say to him/her?' Well, it never fails that if I ask my male students to imagine a hypothetical situation involving their daughter—an imaginary daughter, mind you—they almost immediately become very protective of her, and share that they will go to great lengths to keep her from being hurt. Those lengths always involve inflicting some sort of bodily harm upon their hypothetical daughter's hypothetical suitor. Someone will usually bring up that hilarious scene from a popular movie in which a police detective father and his best friend—also, a detective—try their best to intimidate the young man, who is there to see the daughter for a first date. Pretty funny stuff.

Gentlemen, what I would like to suggest to you is this: In your real-life dealings with young women, remember that she is some guy's daughter. Consider how you would want your daughter to be treated, to be spoken to, to be handled. That should be enough to make you come clean with her about how you really feel—enough to keep you from stringing her along when you know you're not that into her. That should be enough to make you walk away in a heated moment, so that you're not tempted to do something you'll deeply regret later. She's some guy's daughter whether you know that guy or not, and she deserves the same respect you'd want for your daughter. Don't curse at her, don't yell at her, don't beat her down with your words or with your fists. Care for her as you would want your own cared for.

CHAPTER 28
Matters of the Heart

I've had my heart broken a few times, and I guess I've broken a couple, too. I don't believe there was any malice involved—there was certainly none on my part. I just didn't feel about them with the same intensity as they felt about me and vice versa—it happens. Here is what I can tell you about matters of the heart: As much as possible, try to treat people right. If you know you don't like him, don't pretend to like him, because he has a nice car. Don't pretend to like him, so that he can buy things for you. You can earn money and purchase your own items. Don't play with her heart, gentlemen. If you're just not that into her, then you'd better not be into her, understand? People have been shot for less than that—play with it if you want to, but don't say you weren't warned.

Ms. Miller, Do You Have to Say the Pledge in College?

One of my seniors, at that time, asked me that question which I found so innocently cute. 'No,' I responded, 'you won't have to.' The truth is that there will be much in college that you won't have to do. You won't have to attend class, if you choose not to—some students will only go on the first day of class and on test days. You won't have to make your bed or do your laundry, although, I strongly recommend doing both. You won't have to eat your veggies either, but there, again, I think it wise to not consume junk food for every meal. You won't have to have early morning classes, if you don't want them (if you register for classes early enough). Yep, for those of you going off to school, you will find that your college days will offer you the most freedom you have probably ever experienced in your young lives. You will find this newfound independence to be both exciting and at times a little terrifying.

There will be no one to tell you when to get up in the morning, or when to go to bed. No one to manage your money for you; no one to pay your bills for you. No one to caution you against too much partying. No one to tell you that the people you're associating with don't mean you any good. No one to settle disputes between you and your roommate(s)—at different times, I had as many as three at one time. There'll be no one reminding (and in some cases, hounding) you to turn-in assignments, because it won't be your professors' jobs to lead you to water and to make you drink it. In college, you'll be expected to lead yourself to the water.

Ladies, there will be no one to tell you that that dude whispering sweet nothings in your ear was just across campus gassing-up some other young lady's head. Beware. Gentlemen, you, too—be careful. There are some young women out there, who are such good manipulators that they will get you to do their bidding, and make you believe it was your idea to do it in the first place! You'll be thinking you are 'da man.' Yeah, right. Some people leave college with a baby and not a degree—some leave with STDs. Real talk, as I hear some of you say. Facts. Beware.

With all this freedom, it will be imperative that you stay focused on your goal. And this doesn't just hold true for the college-bound—each of you will be faced with these possible distractions. What are your goals? Stay focused. Always, in the back of your mind, as you make decisions, ask yourself if what you are about to do will move you in the direction of achieving your goals. No guy/girl is that fine. Do you hear me? If he can't understand that you need to study for a test—bye! She can't seem to comprehend that you need to put a little more time into your studies this week than into spending time with her—bye!

My first year at the University of Florida, I cried every day. My parents and brother were in Illinois, then, and there was something about knowing that there were hundreds of miles separating us that saddened me. Plus, I was having to make so many decisions for myself—basic things, like what I was going to eat on any given day. Let me also mention that being away at college was the first time in my life that I knew what it was for food to be a luxury item. Seriously.

One of the things that helped to dry the tears I cried that first year was the abundance of good-looking males on that campus. Oh, my word. Ladies, you think there's a guy worth crying over on your campus, or in your neighborhood? Gentlemen, you think there's a young woman worth losing sleep over on your campus? Please. Just, please. Those of you who decide to go off to college, particularly if you're headed to a state university with students from cities all over your state and even from countries around the world, will realize you've been living in a pond when there's a vast ocean out there. You will find yourself trying to figure out what planet produced such fine specimen. Now, everything I've told you about proceeding with caution still applies—just know that the scenery can be especially nice.

Too Late.

Sometimes it's just too late. As high school students, some of you have been given opportunity after opportunity to complete projects and assignments in different classes, or you've been afforded multiple chances to get things right as far as making better choices with your behavior. As a teacher in a high school with young people, who are on the cusp of adulthood and yet, in many ways are still being treated like children, there is a delicate balance between trying to teach you how to be responsible for your actions while attempting to actually keep you accountable for your actions. And I must say, there have been times when school personnel—myself included—have probably done you a disservice, because the reality is that sometimes in life, there is no second chance. Sometimes, it is simply too late. Do all you can while you can. Make that phone call, complete that assignment, take that trip, start that business, write that book, ask for help, have that conversation—do all you can while you can.

Naked and Sexy Are Not Synonymous.

Nakedness does not make you 'sexy'. Your breasts don't need to be fully exposed in order for you to be 'sexy'. Your behind does not need to be exposed, your pecs don't need to be seen, you don't need to bend over, nor do you need to stoop down. Somewhere along the way, hopefully, you will realize that real appeal comes from the confidence in knowing and liking who you are—not from showing more skin. For now, take my word for it and leave a little something to the imagination.

He Said What?!

Don't allow young men to talk to you in any old way. How is it that a young man can, to your face, call you a 'bih'? To your face? When did that become acceptable? And who came up with this shortened version of the word b*tch, anyway? 'Bih.' Is it supposed to be less derogatory—cute even? Ladies, I believe that all the profanity some of you use makes him feel as though you're not worthy of a certain level of respect. When I addressed one young man about it, he told me, "Ms. Miller, that's what they call themselves, so why can't I call them that."

You can disagree, if you want, but I will continue to stand by what I believe and that is this: If you would develop some self-respect, young (and old) ladies, then the young (and old) men in your life would follow suit.

Likewise, where are the men who are examples of how to respectfully communicate with a woman? Where are those men? The ones with standards—the ones not too afraid to stand for something, even though they might end up standing alone. The ones who will call other men on the carpet for their mess—men of integrity. Men who are faithful, men with vocabularies, men who don't feel like profanity makes them cool and tough, so they use it as every other word in a conversation. I'm talking about kind men. Gentlemen who understand that that's where real strength lies. Where are those men?

CHAPTER 29
Coins, Kids, Communication, and College

(Bit)Coins Are Money, Too.

I know people who look down on pennies, as though pennies are second-class money citizens; people who will see a penny on the ground and not pick it up. Ha! Not me—I brake for pennies. Yep, will pick them up and any other coin I may see on the ground. Laugh, if you will—my feelings will not be hurt in the least bit.

Coins are money, too, and I used to share with students that one of the ways in which you can begin saving some money is to not spend your change. I learned that somewhere along the way, and it has worked beautifully. I can't tell you the last time I used coins in a transaction. Neither can some of you, but that's because you use debit and credit cards.

Here's how it works: I purchase an item for $3.10 by giving the cashier a five-dollar bill. The cashier gives me change in the amount of $1.90. I put it in my purse. When I get home, I put the 90 cents into my pink plastic crayon, which is my version of a piggy bank—an empty milk jug will also work. When my crayon is to capacity, I make a trip to the credit union to use their coin-counting machine, and then I deposit that money into a savings account.

Every single time I spend cash, this is what I do. You will be amazed at just how quickly you can accumulate hundreds of dollars. Over the years, I've used my crayon money for everything from treating a friend, who was going through a tough time, to a spur-of-the-moment trip to a major theme park to paying for a title search when purchasing a property. A student shared with me that there's a way to do this electronically with online banking tools. Cool. I just want you to get into the habit of saving some of your money. I recommend getting to the place where you have at least two savings accounts—one where you're saving money for something in particular like a car, or money for your first place; the other for unforeseen circumstances—those things that you couldn't plan for, because you didn't see them coming.

Something that I'm not sure many people saw coming when I first published this book, was cryptocurrency which is digital, or virtual, money. Interesting concept, isn't it? It is being touted, by some, as a way to grow your money by investing in it. I don't know much about it at all, so I can speak neither for nor against it. I do know there are online brokerages, or investment companies where you can buy it as well as buy stock in different companies to invest and grow your money. I heard a financial expert say that no one has ever saved their way to wealth, and while that is probably true, I believe most people could stood stand to save a little more money than they have been saving. And we all can stand to become more financially literate. There are so many ways available to us to learn about any topic imaginable, and money is no exception. Learn more about it. Money has been such a taboo subject with most families that many of us have been learning through trial and error, which can be costly. Search for the knowledge and the information—it's out there.

Who's Bad?

I cringe every time I hear a parent refer to their child as bad. Those of you who have children, don't refer to your little person as that. Children need to hear from their parents that they are bright and kind and loved—not that they're bad. There is a difference between behaving badly and being inherently bad, so be sure to separate the child from their bad behavior. Also, take the time to teach your child how to behave in different places and in certain situations. It is a parent's responsibility to teach their children how to conduct themselves when they're at home and when they're in public. Many of these children being referred to as bad are simply untrained.

Words are very powerful. We have all experienced the power of words. The right words from the right someone can make you feel invincible—hurtful words can make you question your very existence, depending on who said them to you. Remember the power of your words when it comes to your children—people in general, too, but especially when it comes to your children—and be careful what you say to and about them. Don't speak ill of the other parent in their presence. He or she may have been the bane of your existence when you were seeing each other, but they are that child's parent forever. Speak life.

You Have Your Phone Though.

Some of you will come to school with no pen or pencil, no paper—and expect for a teacher to provide you with said supplies—but I have yet to meet a student who forgot to bring their phone. You behave as though those phones are providing you with oxygen. You don't realize that your obsession with them is actually sucking the life out of you. How is it that students never forget to walk with their cellphones? You'll forget to complete your assignments, you'll neglect to bring a writing utensil, you'll show up to class with zero backpack, but lo and behold, your phone is ever present. Why is that? I'll tell you why: You're addicted to those phones like a crackhead is addicted to crack. That's why. Stop it.

And another thing: You are offending people with these electronic devices, and inadvertently closing doors to future opportunities. You have no idea that you're allowing your phone addiction to mess things up for you, so let me help you out. When you go to someone to ask them to do something for you, put the doggone phone away during the conversation. I can tell you from experience that it is incredibly annoying and downright rude for a student to be constantly checking their phone during what is supposed to be a conversation with me. Again, put the doggone phone away. Who the heck are you talking to anyway? Here's how I feel (and I know I'm not alone): If you're talking to me—talk to me. Stop the constant checking of your phone. It's rude.

College or Nah?

With all the talk in schools about college-and-career readiness, let me say this: A college degree doesn't make you better than anyone else. It never has, and it never will. A college degree gives you more choices in life. Training in a particular trade affords you more choices in life. It gives you more options. I want that for everyone, because I don't want for any of you to ever feel that you just have to accept what life decides to offer you. I want you to have choices in life. As difficult as it was some days, college was the right decision for me; it has afforded me a life I don't believe I would have had otherwise. It has, most importantly, afforded me the opportunity to fulfill a part of my purpose in life by being entrusted with teaching young people. The fact that I have a good work ethic plays a definite role, but I must acknowledge the importance of those pieces of paper—the high school diploma, bachelor's degree, and master's degree. Can you have a wonderful life without a degree, or without certification for some type of trade? Yes, but that all depends on the quality of life you want to live.

Pay no attention to those who will attempt to make you feel badly about not going to college; likewise, pay no attention to those who will attempt to make you feel badly for going to college—trust me, they're out there, with their hating selves. Don't be intimidated by people's titles—some worked hard for them, some paid much for them. Don't be intimidated by people with big voices—just because someone says something in a loud voice, doesn't mean they're right. Don't be intimidated by perceived or actual intelligence—the most intelligent person on the planet has insecurities, making them just as human and as flawed as you are. And as intelligent as they may be, there is something you know that they don't; there is some skill you possess that is beyond them. So, when you sit in those rooms with those people, don't be intimidated.

Whatever you decide to do regarding college—whatever action you decide to take—just be prepared to live with the consequences of it, and don't worry about what anyone else has to say about the matter.

CHAPTER 30
Amazing Life, Amazing You

Here Today.

Early one Monday morning, a student asked me if I'd heard what happened. I told her I had not, and she proceeded to tell me about a terrible incident that had taken place Sunday afternoon. A single-car accident—the passenger was dead at the scene and the driver in critical condition at a local hospital.

Just as though it were yesterday, I recall being at the local hospital in the ICU, looking down on a beautiful, former student of mine, and being reminded of just how fleeting life is—we are here one day, and the next it is as though we never existed. Gone. It pained me to see her lying there so still, breathing only with the help of machines. During that same time the year before, she had been preparing for high school graduation, and excited about what was in store.

Learn to live your life in an almost-constant state of gratitude—thankful for the great and for the small things. Be thankful that you've made it thus far—some of you will be the first in your family to earn a high school diploma, to purchase a house, to start a business. Be thankful if you have even one person in your life who cares about you and is cheering you on—count me as one. Be thankful for being able to breathe on your own.

Life Goals.

I had a student tell me one day, 'I just want to be happy.' I understand that—really, I do, but I did encourage the student to begin thinking about what happy meant to her. I say the same to you: Get a picture in your mind about the type of life you want to live. What do you see as your life's work? Where do you see yourself living? Will you marry? Have children? You can make your life what you want it to be. Life doesn't have to just happen to you, but it will take some forethought on your part and some planning—some work and sacrifice, too. If you don't have goals—short-term as well as long-term—you run the risk of life just handing you whatever. Start with today—what do you want to accomplish today? Tomorrow? By next year? Write it down and be about making it happen.

In recent days, I have been asked, 'What do you want?' and do you know that the question sort of had me stumped for a minute? Why? Because I hadn't really considered it in a while. A word I have been hearing since the beginning of this pandemic, has been the word 'pivot' which, in this instance, means to turn and change direction because your circumstances are suddenly no longer the same. Perhaps, one of the most difficult things to deal with is when life ends up not going the way you planned for it to go. You planned to be with that special someone for the rest of your life, and then they decide that a relationship with you is no longer what they want. You planned to work with a certain company, but then the job unexpectedly falls through and you're left trying to figure out your next move. In my own life, things have not exactly followed the path I had in mind for it; circumstances continue to change, and I must again do what I am encouraging you to do—examine your life. Ask yourself *What do I want?* and then, take some time to consider exactly what you want. Write it down and be about it.

Life-long Learning

I realize that not everyone is fond of school—okay, some of you hate it for various reasons, and I can respect your feelings. What I do hope you never grow tired of, though, is learning. You don't have to be in an actual school building to learn; in fact, some of the most meaningful learning I've experienced has been the learning I pursued, because I wanted it. I wasn't being paid to do it, and sometimes I wanted the information so badly I even paid to learn it. I wanted to know something, so I sought out the people who could show me, or the places that could connect me to the knowledge or information I needed. I don't have a problem paying people for access to their expertise, or for the privilege of their time. Knowledge is valuable—it can take you to the next level in your business, in your relationship, in your personal development as a human. You should have no qualms about investing in yourself. You are so worth it!

One of the things I am particularly aware of lately is the importance of being around like-minded people, so I am intentionally seeking out others who are striving toward some of the same goals. It's important to be around others whose conversation is on that next level as opposed to those same old discussions being had by the small-minded. Haven't you ever known in your heart-of-hearts that you just couldn't continue to do what you had been used to doing, especially if you wanted some other better things in your life? Here's a quote for you: If you always do what you've always done, then you'll always have what you've always had.

Long after formal schooling—whether that's high school or trade school or university—you should still be learning new things. Read a book, talk to different people, search the internet, watch a documentary, visit a new place. Learning is growing and should be a life-long pursuit.

Amazing You.

Of all the lessons shared in this book, I hope the one that most stands out to you is that you are nothing short of amazing. I think you should practice saying aloud, *I'm amazing.* If you're like me, then you probably don't celebrate yourself nearly enough. I think you should start now by confidently proclaiming, *I'm amazing.*

The truth is that you are, at this very moment, the solution to somebody's problem. You are the answer to somebody's question. The head of some corporation is somewhere right now scratching her head, trying to figure out what to do and here you are the answer—with your amazing self. Some brand-new innovation is waiting to be birthed, and you are its inventor. You are capable. You are enough. You are brilliant and up to the task. You are needed. You are amazing.

So, do it, make it happen, go after it, create it, speak it, fix it, sing it, change it, learn it, organize it, invest in it, write it, give it, apply for it, lead it, rise above it, design it, visit it, sell it, dream it, live it.

May you realize your full potential as a human being—leaving no unexplored, gifts and talents behind when it comes time to exit this life. May you continue to overcome adversity in your life. May you question and fight against the injustices of this world. May you be an example to others of what is possible when good triumphs. May you never stop learning and improving and growing. May you never stop dreaming, and never stop working toward your goals. May you discover and fulfill your purpose in life. ☺

Discussion Questions

Chapter 1:

1. The author believes that students need lessons on how to manage life, but aren't schools already doing that? What do you think and why?
2. Some people are satisfied with working for someone else for their whole life, and then retiring. And then, there are some who want to be their own boss and have their own business. Which do you think you are and why?

Chapter 2:

3. In what areas of your life do you tend to compare yourself to others? Which qualities do you personally struggle with the most (looks, athleticism, intelligence…)?
4. Why do you think we are so prone to comparing ourselves to others? Do you agree that women are even more likely to do so, especially with aspects of physical beauty? If so, why?
5. Everything you could possibly want in this life comes with a price. Everything. Do you agree or disagree? Do you have any examples from your own life of things that have cost you (time, money, sweat, tears...)?
6. What are the negative effects of living a competitive life? Are there any positive effects? If so, what are they?
7. Are you genuinely happy for people in your life when

good things happen to them? If you are not, how can you change your perspective for the better?
8. What does it mean to be content?
9. Do you consider yourself to be a content person? Why or why not?
10. There is always someone worse off than you. Do you agree with this statement? Why or why not?
11. Ms. Miller suggests that you do your best to succeed at running your own race. How exactly do we do that?

Chapter 3:

12. It's a beautiful thing when your teacher/professor/employer/mother-in-law actually cares about you, but it is not a prerequisite to you doing what you need to do. Do you agree with the quote? Why or why not?
13. How does the author suggest we deal with people who don't like us? Is this how you already deal with people like that, or should you change your ways?

Chapter 5:

14. There is more to sex than meets the eye. Do you agree? Why or why not?
15. Do you agree with the author's assertion that some people are cookie monsters? Support your answer.
16. Overall, do you agree with the author's opinions on the topic of sex? What do you not agree with? Why do you not agree with it?

Chapter 6:

17. One of the reasons that Ms. Miller gives for speaking to *everybody* is the fact that you never know who you are going to need in this life. Do you have any per-

sonal stories that would support this claim?

Chapter 7:

18. You can also be unhappy with money. Do you agree? Why or why not?
19. Money is a tool to be used. Do you agree? Why or why not?
20. Are you letting the pursuit of money consume you? What kinds of things do people do when they do these things? What is the evidence in your life that you are (or are not) worshiping money?
21. People who really have money are often the humblest, most unassuming people you'd ever hope to meet. Do you agree with this? If so, can you think of any examples?

Chapter 8:

22. What kinds of problems do you want to help solve? What could be your next step toward moving in that direction?
23. The author encourages you to find out what you were put on this earth to do. Do you know yet? If so, how do you know?
24. How important is having a purpose in this life to you? Why is it important?
25. Your purpose in life always involves doing something with or providing something for others. Do you agree? Why or why not?
26. What are your gifts and talents? How can they benefit you and others?

Chapter 9:

27. If you're not careful, you're going to waste your life away on your electronic devices. What do you think about this warning?
28. Do you believe that phones and the internet addictive? Why or why not?
29. If technology can, in fact, be addictive, what steps are you taking to ensure that you are not a victim?
30. Do you need rehab?

Chapter 10:

31. What is one of the first things that Ms. Miller tells her students? Why do you think she is more emphatic about her directive concerning people who do not look like her?
32. There is a long history of hatred attached to that name. Do you know anything (historically or personally) about this? Please explain.
33. Why does Ms. Miller not agree with those people who argue that the term is now one of endearment?
34. Why do you think it is most disheartening to the author when she hears black students refer to each other by using the word? Do you personally use the term? If so, why do you use it?

Chapter 11:

35. Do you agree with Ms. Miller's statement that giving freely and willingly from the heart is one of the greatest feelings in the world? Why or why not?
36. Why shouldn't we give looking for praise or some sort of favor in return?
37. What does Ms. Miller mean exactly by learning how

not to give? Can you relate at all to this concept?
38. Why do you think that Ms. Miller shared the paper route story? Do you have a similar story? If so, share it!

Chapter 12:

39. Why doesn't your story have to look like everybody else's story?
40. What are the advantages to buying a car (or even a house) outright?
41. What does the author mean by buying under the influence? Are you susceptible to the same thing? Why or why not?

Chapter 13:

42. According to Ms. Miller, what often happens to children who do not read much? Do you agree? Can you relate to this statement personally? Do you know anyone who has been affected in this way?
43. The ability to read, and to read well is huge. Do you agree? Why or why not?
44. Do you think that you will foster a love for reading in your children when you are a parent? Why or why not?

Chapter 14:

45. Why do we feel like giving up when life knocks us down with what sometimes feels like a kick in the chest?

46. There's a strength that comes in the going. I know what I'm talking about. What do you think the author

means?
47. What does Ms. Miller mean by "there is life after a failure"? Do you believe this to be true? Why or why not?
48. What are your thoughts about seeing a counselor if you need to? Under what circumstances would you seek the help of a counselor?

Chapter 15:

49. What is Ms. Miller's advice about use of social media? Do you agree with her? Why or why not? Have you used social media inappropriately?
50. How do you feel about what is or is not appropriate behavior?
51. Why do you think that there are young people today who think that it is okay for a man to put his hands on a woman in an aggressive or violent manner?
52. Ms. Miller believes that women should also keep their hands to themselves. What do you think? Support your answer.
53. Do you agree that most women often find themselves attracted to men like their fathers? Why or why not?
54. No matter how much you love a person and wish for them to make better decisions, they have to want better for themselves. Do you agree with this statement? Why or why not?
55. How might distancing ourselves from a loved one who is living a destructive life help the situation?
56. Have you found yourself trying to control anyone lately? Why?
57. Does it matter how we respond to other people in our lives? How does it matter?

Chapter 16:

58. Showing appreciation is what makes people want to continue giving to you and looking out for you. Do you agree with this? Why or why not?
59. Ms. Miller talks about the fact that no one owes us anything. Do you think that people owe you anything or that you are entitled to anything? If so, who or what?
60. Ms. Miller expands the notion of gratitude as something that needs to be taught. Why does gratitude need to be taught? Do you agree with her on this point?
61. Is it ever okay to call someone a b*tch? Support your answer.

Chapter 17:

62. The thought that dark skin is somehow inferior is prevalent in many parts of the world—where did that thought come from? What effect might that belief have on someone with a dark complexion? What effect might that same belief have on someone with a light complexion?

Chapter 19:

63. Why does the author seem to be so adamant about buying a house? Do you agree?

Chapter 21:

64. What have you done that was outside of your comfort zone? How did it feel after you did it?
65. According to the author, why is it important for us to do things that scare us? What are the risks? What are the benefits?

Chapter 23:

66. Name some places you would like to visit and why.

Chapter 25:

67. The author believes that it cannot feel good to be in a 'baby mama' situation. What do you think?

Chapter 26:

68. Was Ms. Miller overreacting about the guy who showed up at the store after she told him not to? Explain.
69. When you consider your life—next year, five years, and even ten years from now—what do you want?

Chapter 27:

70. How do you believe unwanted touches should be handled?
71. How might your friends provide a pretty accurate glimpse into your future? Do you believe you should seek out different circles of friends for different interests?

Chapter 29:

72. A college degree doesn't make you better than anyone else. Do you agree with this statement? Why or why not?
73. Can you have a wonderful life without a degree? If so, how would you define/describe a wonderful life?
74. The author says that whatever you decide to do – whatever action you decide to take – just be prepared to live with the consequences of it. Are you prepared to live with the consequences of your decisions? How

do you know?

Chapter 30:

75. The author believes that learning should be a lifelong pursuit. What do you think? What do you want to learn more about?
76. Did you say aloud *I'm amazing*? How did it feel to say it, and why do you suppose that is? Why would the author suggest saying it?
77. If you didn't know it before, now that you know you're amazing, what are your next steps?

www.ingramcontent.com/pod-product-compliance
Lightning Source LLC
LaVergne TN
LVHW051841080426
835512LV00018B/2996